Lone Star Legends

presents

# David Crockett

by

Robert E. Hollmann

DURBAN HOUSE

Printed in the United States of America.

For information address:
Durban House Publishing Company, Inc.
7502 Greenville Avenue, Suite 500, Dallas, Texas 75231

Library of Congress Cataloging-in-Publication Data
Hollmann, Robert E., 1944 –

David Crockett / Robert E. Hollmann

Library of Congress Control Number: 2004117834

p. cm.

ISBN 1-930754-75-2
First Edition

10  9  8  7  6  5  4  3  2  1

Visit our Web site at
http://www.durbanhouse.com

*To Addison and Dylan White*

*Addie and Dylan*

*Two Great Grandchildren*

# Acknowledgements

I want the thank Jeri Gandy, Ann Ellison and the ladies of the Daughters of the Republic of Texas, Presidents of Texas Chapter, for all their assistance and encouragement in the writing of this book. I want to thank Ben Ellison of Benjamin's Photography for the photograph. Alicia Johnson has done a lot to promote the book. Tammie Sanchez has done a lot of work to get the book ready to publish. Thanks to my publisher, John Lewis, for taking a chance on this project. I want to thank my daughter, Carrie, for her work in promoting this book. Addison and Dylan White, my grandchildren, were the inspiration for two of the characters in the book. As always, thanks to my daughters, Kristina and Kasey, for all they do. And to my son, Rob, who makes me proud. My wife, Katie, is always there for me and I couldn't do this without her encouragement and support. Thanks to these and to all who support me in my effort to take Texas history to the children of Texas.

*Robert E. Hollmann*
*Odessa, Texas*
*December 2004*

*Be always sure you are right,*
*then go ahead*

— David Crockett

# David Crockett

# Chapter
# One

"ALL RIGHT CLASS, PAY ATTENTION PLEASE." Ms. Julianne Johnson, teacher of the fourth grade class at David Crockett Elementary school in Eden Prairie, Texas, tapped her ruler on her desk. "I have an assignment for you that will be due on Monday."

A groan went up from the students seated in the classroom. Addie turned to her friends, Dylan and Braden, and rolled her eyes. She wanted to have fun this weekend, not do an assignment.

"Addie." Ms. Johnson's voice caused Addie to turn her head back toward the teacher. "Do you have something you want to tell the whole class?"

Addie looked down at her desk. "No, Ms. Johnson."

"Very well." Ms. Johnson walked in front of her desk and faced the class. "This month we celebrate Texas Independence Day. I think it would be good for us to learn something about the man that this school is named for. So by Monday, I want you to have a paper prepared that tells about the life of David Crockett. I will let you work in teams. On Monday you will present the paper to the class."

Dylan put his head in his hands, and Braden twirled his pencil. They wanted to play ball this weekend. Now they would have to work on this assignment. Ms. Johnson handed out some papers to the class. "This will give you an idea of how to write the paper. The group that writes the best paper and makes the best presentation will win a surprise."

The bell ending the class rang as Addie took the paper from Ms. Johnson. She looked over the paper then stuffed it in her backpack. She picked up her books and hurried after Dylan and Braden. She caught up with them as they walked down the hall.

"Hey, guys. Want to work on the paper together?"

Braden looked at Addie. "I don't want to work

on it at all." He walked a little further then turned to her. "But I guess we have to do it, so why not? What do you think, Dylan?"

"Sure. Got any ideas how we can find out some good information? If we have to do this then we might as well try to win the surprise."

"I have an idea," Addie said. "I'll get my mother to take us to the Alamo tomorrow. She's going to San Antonio and we can look around there while she does her shopping."

Braden stopped walking. "What do you think we are going to find at the Alamo?"

Addie shook her head. "I don't know. I've heard that there are ghosts there. Maybe we can find one and ask him about David Crockett."

"I thought his name was Davy," Dylan said.

Addie walked toward her mother's car. "We can ask the ghost that too. I'll see you in the morning," she called over her shoulder.

Braden and Dylan watched her get into the car. Dylan turned to Braden. "Well, I guess I'll see you tomorrow. Better get some rest if we are going to hunt for ghosts."

"Now, children." Addie's mother leaned her head out of the open window of her car. "I will be back in a couple of hours. Don't go anywhere else. I will pick you up right here."

Addie waved at her mother. "Okay, Mom. We will be right here."

The children watched the car drive away then turned and walked toward the Alamo.

"What's the plan?" Braden asked.

Addie shrugged her shoulders. "I don't know. I thought we could look around. Maybe we can find something that will make our report the best."

Dylan rolled his eyes. "You don't know? We wasted a whole day coming here when you don't have any plan except looking for ghosts. I don't know why I listen to you, Addie."

Addie stuck her tongue out at Dylan. "You listen to me because you don't have a better plan. Well, let's go inside and look around."

The three friends entered the Alamo chapel and spent some time looking around. They walked around the grounds and wandered through the gift shop. They had not found anything to help them write their report so far. They were sitting on the grass next to an old cannon.

"Well, now we're going to have to spend all day

tomorrow writing our report with no new information."
Braden threw a pebble at a cup lying in the grass.

"Yes. Thanks for wasting our day, Addie," Dylan said.

"What's that?" Addie got up and walked over to an old building hidden by some trees. Braden and Dylan followed her.

"Just an old building. Doesn't look like anybody's been in it for a long time," Braden said.

Addie pushed on the door and it slowly swung open. She started to walk in, but Dylan grabbed her arm.

"What are you doing? You can't go in there. There's no telling what's in there."

Addie pulled away from Dylan. "What's wrong? Afraid? I thought you didn't believe in ghosts. Well, you two can stay out here, but I'm going to see what's inside. Who knows, it might be just what we're looking for."

Addie walked into the old building. Dylan and Braden looked at each other then followed her in. The building was dark, but the light from the open door allowed them to see some of the room. Just as the friends cleared the door, it slammed shut behind them. They all jumped at the loud noise.

"Why did you shut the door?" Addie asked. "Now we can't see anything."

"I didn't shut it," Braden said.

"Me either." Dylan turned around. "Let's get out of here."

Addie stared hard trying to get her eyes to adjust to the darkness of the room.

"Just a minute," she said. She walked a little further into the room and peered into a corner. "I thought I heard something."

All three children listened, and soon they heard the sound of footsteps softly coming toward them. Soon they could make out a dark shape standing in front of them. The friends huddled together against the wall.

"Who's there?" Addie asked.

The voice of the dark shape filled the small room. "My name's David Crockett."

# Chapter Two

THE THREE CHILDREN STARED IN SHOCKED SILENCE at the dark figure. Finally Addie stammered, "Did you say David Crockett?"

The figure nodded. "That's right. Who are you and what are you doing in here?"

Addie walked slowly toward the dark figure. Her eyes were adjusting to the darkness of the room. She saw a tall man dressed in a buckskin suit with a coonskin cap perched on his head. He leaned on a long rifle. Even in the dimly lit room, Addie could tell he had a kind face and a twinkle in his eye.

"My name is Addie." She stuck out her hand. "These are my two friends, Dylan and Braden. We have to do a paper on you for school, and we came here to try and find some good information on your life."

Crockett laughed softly as he took her hand. "You're doing a story on my life for school. Don't that beat all."

Dylan walked over and stood by Addie. "Yes sir. Our school is named David Crockett Elementary School."

Crockett laughed louder. "Named a school for me, did they? I guess they didn't look up my school record."

"Mr. Crockett." Braden looked up at the tall man. "I always thought your name was Davy. But it seems like everybody calls you David. Which is it?"

"Well you see, my given name is David. I used that for a long time. But then when I started getting known in some parts and got elected to Congress, there was an actor who made up a character based on me called Nimrod Wildfire. It seems this Wildfire character did all sorts of amazing things. Hunting bears, fighting Indians, taming animals. Why, it got so that people couldn't tell the difference between him and me. They thought that David was too formal for such a man, so they started calling me Davy. You can call me what you want. I'll answer to most anything."

Addie looked at her hand that Crockett's still held. "Are you a ghost? You don't feel like a ghost."

Crockett let go of Addie's hand. "Well, Addie, I don't reckon I'm actually a ghost. More like a spirit. I don't haunt this place. I come back here from time to time and watch what's going on. Mostly I come at night when there's nobody here. I walk around and remember what happened here all those many years ago."

"Could you tell us about yourself?" Dylan asked.

"You think folks would really like to know about me?"

All the children nodded.

"Well now, let's see. I was born in Greene County, Tennessee back in 1786. I had a pretty good time growing up. I played in the woods a lot and learned about animals and plants. I never had much school learning. I skipped school once and thought sure I would get a licking, so I ran away from home. I worked for a man driving cattle to Virginia. It was hard work, but I got to see a lot of nice country. When we got to Virginia I found several jobs. It was over two years before I got back to my family."

"Gosh, Davy. Weren't you afraid to be by yourself, no family or anything?" Braden asked.

"Yeah." Dylan joined in. "I would hate to be away

from my family for so long."

Davy looked into the gloom as if seeing something from long ago. "Oh, I missed them, all right. But I was learning a lot too. Things about getting along with people that would help me later. I borrowed my employer's gun and learned to shoot; I became a pretty good shot. Why, I even earned enough to buy my own rifle...and a horse. I started entering shooting contests. We would shoot at targets, and the best shot would win a quarter of beef. Why, some contests I won all four beef quarters. We ate real good in those days."

Addie walked around the room. "How did you get into this room?"

"I have my secret way. I'll show you if you like."

Addie clapped her hands. "Oh, yes. I want to see your secret way."

"Hold on, Addie." Braden looked at the door. "We have to meet your mother pretty soon. Maybe we should just listen to Davy's story and go on."

"Yeah, if I'm late for supper my mom will be real mad," Dylan said.

"Well, I want to see the secret way. Will it take very long?"

Davy shook his head. "No. It won't take long. In fact, where we are going I will be able to show you my life story. You can watch what is happening, but no one will be able to see or hear you."

"What fun," Addie cried. "That will be so much better that reading a book we have read before. We can see what really happened, and then our story will win the surprise."

Braden looked around. "How do we get there? People will see us if we go outside."

Davy chuckled. "We won't go outside. My way is not only secret. It is magic. Nobody will see us. We can come back whenever you want. But I think you will have a good time."

"How do we get there?" Addie asked.

Davy held out his hand. "Take my hand. You two grab on too. We all hold hands and then we walk toward that wall."

Dylan reached for Addie's hand. "We are going to walk into the wall?"

Braden grabbed Dylan's hand. "I don't think it's real smart to walk into the wall."

Davy smiled. "Just come with me. Are you ready?" He looked at the three faces staring up at him. They all nodded. "Well then, hold on tight and let's go."

The three children squeezed their hands tightly and walked beside Davy toward the wall. As they approached the wall, a circle of light appeared, and they could see green fields and trees on the other side.

"Wow," Braden said. "Look at that. Where are we going?"

# Chapter
# Three

Davy led the three friends down a tunnel of light. Shortly they emerged into a green hillside. Addie turned around, but the tunnel of light was gone. She turned back and looked down the valley that stretched below them. A river wound its way through the valley. Trees grew thickly on the hillside and in the valley.

"Man, this is really pretty." Braden shaded his eyes as he looked around.

"It sure is a lot different from Eden Prairie." Dylan took a deep breath. "Air smells good too."

"Where's Davy?" Addie looked around her, but

Davy was gone.

The boys looked around too. "I don't know," Dylan said. "He was right here with us."

"What are we going to do?" Braden asked.

"Let's walk down to the valley. I bet somebody lives down there. Maybe they know where Davy lives." Addie started to walk away.

"Wait a minute." Dylan called out. "Davy said nobody could see or hear us."

Addie shrugged her shoulders. "Oh well. We'll just have to listen and learn where we need to go. Davy brought us here. I think he had a reason." She started walking down the hill. Dylan and Braden followed her, and soon they were kneeling on the river bank, drinking the cool, clear water.

Addie stood up and wiped her mouth. "Look over there." She pointed above the trees. "There's some smoke. Let's go see what it is."

Dylan shook his head. "What if it's Indians?"

Addie smiled. "They can't see us. Remember? Come on. If we're going to get a story, we need to find Davy." She walked away and the boys followed her.

Soon they came to a clearing in the forest. A log cabin sat in the middle of the clearing. The children stayed behind the trees and watched the cabin. Soon the door opened and Davy walked out. He had his cap on and carried his rifle. A pretty dark haired woman walked by his side.

"When will you be back, Davy?" she asked.

"Soon as I get us some meat for supper, Polly. I don't think it will take too long. There's a lot of game in this forest. Do you have something special you want?"

"Some deer would be nice. I could make a stew. Or maybe a turkey. I'm baking some bread to go with whatever you bring back."

Davy leaned down and kissed her on the cheek. "Have the kids help you today. Don't let them just play all day."

"Don't worry, Davy. They help me a lot. Hurry back."

"I'll be home before dark." Davy walked away, turned and waved then disappeared into the forest. Polly watched him walk into the forest, then went back inside the cabin.

The friends were watching Davy and Polly so closely that they did not hear the footsteps coming up behind them.

"Want to go hunting?" Davy asked.

The unexpected sound of his voice made all the children jump. They lay on the grass breathing heavily and looking up at Davy. At last Addie found her voice.

"How did you get here? We saw you just walk

into the woods over there."

Davy laughed. "Sometimes I move fast. Come on. We've got food to find."

The children followed Davy down a forest path. The tall trees blocked out most of the sunlight and it was cool in the woods, even though the sun was shining. Davy did not talk as he led them deeper into the woods. He moved quietly and turned his head from side to side watching for any sign of game. None of the children talked as they followed Davy. They watched him and were surprised how quietly he moved down the trail. Suddenly Davy stopped and looked up into a tree. The children looked up and saw a raccoon clinging to a branch and staring down at the group. Davy raised his rifle and pointed it at the raccoon. The children put their hands over their ears in expectation of the rifle's blast.

Davy slowly lowered his rifle. He gazed at the raccoon and began to grin at the animal. Addie, Dylan, and Braden lowered their hands from their ears and watched as Davy continued to grin at the raccoon. The raccoon seemed surprised as he stared back at Davy. For several minutes the raccoon looked down at the frontiersman who grinned up at him. Finally he climbed to another branch, found his way to another tree and disappeared. Davy watched him go, then shook his head in disappointment.

"What's wrong, Davy?" Braden asked.

"Oh, I got this idea that I can grin an animal down. I've tried it on squirrels, rabbits, and now this raccoon. It doesn't seem to work. Well, let's get to hunting. There's going to be some hungry folks at home tonight."

Later Davy led the friends back down the trail toward his cabin. A deer was slung over his shoulder, and some rabbits were tied at his belt. When they came to the clearing, they saw that there were some men standing outside Davy's cabin talking to Polly. She didn't look very happy.

"Should we stay here, Davy?" Dylan asked.

"No. Come on. They can't see you. Let's find out what's going on."

Davy walked across the clearing toward the men. Addie and the two boys followed him. "Hello, boys," he called out. "What's going on?"

One of the men walked toward him. "Glad you're back, Davy. We need you to come with us."

Davy set the deer down on the ground. "Where are we going, Amos?"

Amos looked over at Polly, then back at Davy. "The Red Sticks have gone on the warpath. All the men are meeting in town to go fight them. We need you to join us."

Davy looked down at the children, who were

staring wide-eyed at him.

"Well, friends. Looks like you're going to have a good story to write for your school."

# Chapter Four

THE THREE FRIENDS WALKED BESIDE DAVY as he marched with the column of soldiers heading deeper and deeper into the forest. Some of the men sang or whistled or talked to each other as they walked along, but Davy was silent. Braden turned to Addie.

"What's wrong with Davy? He hasn't said a word since we left."

Addie looked at Davy's face. He had a little smile on his lips, and his eyes were half closed. "I think he's thinking about home," she said. "About his wife and children. He sure hated to leave them this morning."

Dylan tripped over a tree root. He got up and brushed himself off. "Well, why did he leave? This walking all day is no fun. This forest has too many trees. I'm ready to get back to Eden Prairie."

Davy looked down at the three children. "You're right. I miss my family. I wish I was home with them right now. But sometimes a man has to do things to make a better place for his family to live. I want my family to be safe, so I have to leave them for a while to get rid of dangers to them."

"Do you like to fight?" Braden asked.

Davy shook his head. "No. I don't like to fight. I wish everybody could get along with each other. But, because I love my family, I am willing to fight for them."

Davy smiled. "And then when I come home, I'll get some big hugs and we'll have us a party."

"What will you do at your party?" Addie asked.

"Why, we'll cook a big dinner. Then afterward, we'll sing some songs, maybe dance a little, and I'll play my fiddle."

"You can play the fiddle?" Dylan asked. "I wish I could. I am going to take violin lessons this summer. Would you play for us sometime?"

"Sure I will. Tonight when we camp, I'll play you some real loud tunes. Why we'll have those Indians dancing to the music, and they'll be so happy they won't want to fight anymore."

The column moved on and finally the captain gave the order to stop for the night. Addie, Dylan, and Braden watched as the men set up the camp. Soon fires were blazing and the smell of roasting meat filled the air. The sun was setting as the men finished eating. Most of them lay back on the ground around the fires and talked. Finally one of the men called to Davy. "Hey, Davy. How about giving us a tune on your fiddle?"

Davy thought for a minute. "I reckon we are far enough away that the Indians won't hear us," he said.

Davy stood up and walked over to his bag. He reached in and pulled out a fiddle. He tuned it up and then began to play a song. Soon all the men were clapping their hands in time with the music. A few men stood up and began to stomp around. The music got faster, and the dancers kept up with it. Soon it was so fast that the dancing men were twirling like tops. Finally Davy stopped playing and the men fell to the ground, gasping for air while the rest of the camp roared with laughter.

"Wow," Braden said. "That was some tune. Do you know any more?"

Davy nodded. "I sure do. I know lots of tunes." He looked at the dancers lying on the ground, gasping for air. "But I don't know if they could stand another one right now."

Addie looked up through the trees. She could see the moon shining and the stars twinkling in the night sky.

"This is sure pretty here, Davy. I see why you love this place so much."

"Yes. This is as pretty a place as God ever made. But there are lots of pretty places. Why, I hear that west of here, there are lands that go on forever. Herds of deer and buffalo. Land just there for the taking. Someday I plan to go and explore that land. I want to know if it is as nice as everybody says it is."

Dylan yawned and Davy noticed that the men were getting their bedrolls ready to go to sleep.

"Guess we better get some sleep. I think we're going to have a busy day tomorrow."

Addie and the others lay on the soft ground. They listened to the sounds of the night. A dove cooed and another answered. Some unseen animal crashed its way through the thick brush that grew near the campsite. Addie watched as a cloud drifted across the face of the moon cloaking everything in darkness. Then it just as quickly moved away, and the moonlight bathed the sleeping camp in its shimmering light. She wondered what the next day would hold for them. Soon she began

# David Crockett

to feel very sleepy. Before long she was sound asleep, along with Braden and Dylan. In the whole camp only one figure was awake. Davy sat staring into the embers of the fire. He was thinking about his home and family and about how badly he wished he were with them.

# Chapter
# Five

THE THREE CHILDREN WOKE UP to the sounds of the camp getting ready to move out. They rubbed the sleep from their eyes and stood up. Davy walked over to them and handed each one a piece of bacon and a piece of hard bread.

"Good morning," he said cheerily. "Are you ready to be moving out?"

Braden looked around at the men falling into line. "Where are we going?" he asked.

Davy pointed down the trail. "About five miles that way, there's an Indian village. It is the one whose

# David Crockett

warriors attacked the settlers the other day. We are going to march to that village."

Dylan started to say something, but an order to fall in was shouted. Davy motioned for the children to follow him and found his place in the line of soldiers. The sun was shining and soon Addie and her friends were sweating as they walked alongside of Davy.

It felt like they had marched for hours when the command to halt was given. They looked down the trail but were unable to see anything. Some officers came walking down the trail taking men with them and disappearing into the woods. At last an officer approached Davy and motioned him to follow. They walked into the forest and followed the officer as he led them to an opening in the trees. In a clearing was an Indian village. The soldiers stayed out of sight in the trees as they waited for word to attack.

Addie, Dylan and Braden watched the activity in the camp. Women cooked over open fires while children played around the huts. Dogs sat near the cooking fires in hopes of getting scraps of food. Several men lay around the camp talking and smoking their pipes. Addie thought the scene was like any other family scene. She felt sad when she thought about the coming battle.

A shot was fired on the other side of the camp. Soon all the soldiers were shooting and yelling as they ran toward the Indian camp. The Indians were caught completely by surprise. Women ran screaming through the camp looking for their children. Warriors rushed into their tents to find weapons to meet the attack. Dogs barked and children looked for somewhere to hide. Smoke from the rifles became so thick that it was hard to see. The children's nostrils burned from the smell of gunpowder. They stayed back in the woods and watched the fight.

Soon the fighting stopped. The smoke cleared away and the friends saw a group of Indians surrounded by soldiers. Addie, Braden, and Dylan walked down to the camp and stood beside Davy. He leaned on his rifle as he watched the Indians. One of the officers walked up to Davy and said something to him. Davy nodded then walked over and stood in front of the frightened Indians.

"Howdy. My name's David Crockett. Who is your chief?"

A tall man with eagle feathers in his hair walked out of the group and stood before Davy.

"My name is Red Star. I am the chief of this band."

Davy stuck out his hand. "Glad to meet you, Red Star. My friends and I came here because your warriors attacked a settlement last week. We want to live in peace, but we must protect our homes."

"As must we," said Red Star as he shook Davy's hand. "The white chief told us we could live on these lands forever. Now white settlers are moving onto the lands and taking them from the Indians. We must protect our homes also."

Davy nodded. "Yes, you must. We did not know of the white settlers taking your lands. When I get back home, I will go to the government and have them remove the settlers from your lands."

Red Star looked puzzled. "You will do this for us?"

Davy smiled. "Sure as my name's David Crockett. I give you my word and I give you my hand that as long as I am able, I will do everything I can to see you get to keep your home."

"Then I give you my word and my hand that as long as the settlers stay off our land, there will be peace."

Davy smiled. "Sounds like we have a deal. Now Red Star, this marching and fighting has made me hungry. Do you think your tribe can rustle up some food for us before we start back?"

Several hours later, Addie, Dylan, and Braden walked beside Davy as they headed for his cabin.

"Gosh, Davy," Dylan said. "I can't believe that the Indians would be so ready to make peace with you."

Davy stopped and looked back toward the Indian village. "Dylan, they're just folks like anybody else. They love their homes and their families and want to protect them, just like I would. I meant what I said about doing what I can to help them keep their land."

"Davy, are you going to run for the legislature like the men talked about?" Braden asked.

Davy turned around and started walking. "I don't know. I'll think about it. Right now I just want to get home and see my wife and family. I guess tomorrow will take care of itself."

# Chapter Six

ADDIE, DYLAN, AND BRADEN SAT UNDER A TREE and watched as Davy paced back and forth in front of the cabin door. They had never seen Davy look so worried. Inside the cabin a doctor and some of the local women were taking care of Polly. She had become sick and Davy had sent for the doctor, but she did not seem to be getting any better. Davy stopped his pacing and leaned against the wall of the cabin. His eyes were closed, and his lips moved in a silent prayer.

"I wish there was something we could do for him," Braden whispered to Addie.

"So do I," she replied. "He looks so sad."

The door to the cabin opened and the doctor

walked out. He was drying his hands on a towel. He walked over to Davy and put his hand on his shoulder. Davy looked at the doctor with hope in his eyes.

"I'm sorry, Davy. We did all we could. She was just too sick. I'm afraid she is gone."

Davy's shoulders slumped. He leaned against the wall to keep from falling to the ground. He lifted his head and tried to speak, but no words came from his mouth. Addie saw a tear fall from his eye and run down his cheek. For several moments everyone was silent. Finally, Davy brushed the tear from his cheek and straightened up. He looked at the doctor.

"Thank you for all you did for her." He put out his hand, and the doctor took it. "I would like to see her alone now."

The doctor called the women who had been assisting him outside. The children watched as Davy walked into the house and closed the door. A while later, Davy came outside. His eyes were red, but he forced a smile.

"I will bury her on that little hill overlooking the valley. It was her favorite place. Once again, thank you all."

The day of Polly's funeral was cloudy, and a soft rain fell. The preacher gave a short service, and the neighbors, who had come to the funeral, all gave their support to Davy. When the service was over and the people had left, Davy walked around inside the empty cabin. He seemed to be hearing laughter and voices from happier days. Finally he walked out of the cabin into the rain and headed to the woods. The children hurried after him. He walked deep into the forest and finally stopped under a giant tree. He sat down and leaned back against the tree trunk. Addie and the boys sat down next to him and waited for him to speak. After several minutes, Dylan spoke up.

"What are you going to do now, Davy?"

Davy looked at the children as if he did not know they were there.

"I don't know. I think I'll just pack my gear and head off into the forest. I'll live out here and I won't have anybody to bother me."

"You can't do that," Braden said.

"And why can't I?" Davy asked.

Braden looked at Davy. "A lot of people look up to you. They are counting on you to help make this country a safe place to live."

"He's right, Davy," Addie said. "You can make this a better place to live for a lot of people."

Davy shook his head and looked down at the ground.

"Why do I care if this is a better place for other

people to live? What makes you think I could do anything to make this better anyway?"

Dylan got up and walked over and stood in front of Davy.

"Because you are Davy Crockett. And nobody can do the things you can do. I know you are sad right now, but tomorrow I think you will believe that you should help make this country better. Remember what you told the Indians? They are trusting in you too. You have a lot to offer everyone, and you can't do it if you are hiding in the forest."

Addie reached over and took his hand. "Davy, whether you like it or not, people look up to you and count on you. You don't have a choice. You are Davy Crockett."

Davy looked at the children.

"Yes, I'm Davy Crockett. I wish I was David Crockett, because he could walk off into the forest and forget everything. But this Davy, he is the one that has to help people and make something of this country." He stood up and brushed off his pants. "So, I guess that Davy needs to get back. I believe there is an election to win."

# Chapter
# Seven

THE CAMPAIGN WAS A SUCCESS, and Davy was elected to the state legislature. He worked hard to pass bills that would permit settlers to have new land, while at the same time he kept his promise to the Indians that they could keep their homes.

Davy worked hard, and when he had a chance, he liked to go hunting in the nearby forests and hills. One day while he was out hunting, he found the track of a large bear. Addie, Dylan, and Braden watched as Davy followed the track for several miles. Suddenly he stopped and the children saw a cave in the side of a small mountain.

Davy slowly walked toward the cave, being careful to stay hidden in the trees. When he got to the edge of a clearing, he stopped and watched the cave. The children sat next to Davy and did not say a word. After a while, the bear walked out of the cave and sniffed the air. Davy slowly raised the gun to his shoulder and prepared to fire. Before he could pull the trigger, three bear cubs came tumbling out of the cave. They ran to their mother and playfully tugged at her. Davy slowly lowered his rifle and slipped quietly back into the woods. The children followed him and when they were away from the cave, Braden walked beside Davy.

"Why didn't you shoot that bear? It would have made a nice rug."

Davy put his hand on Braden's head. "Those cubs need a mother much more than I need a rug. One thing you should remember is that you should never kill something for no reason. All God's creatures have a right to live. That bear had a family to take care of. It would not be right to take her from her family for no reason except I want something to put on my floor."

The children followed Davy back to his room. When they got there, they found several men waiting for them.

"Davy, glad you are back." One of the men stuck

out his hand to Davy. "We have something we want to talk to you about."

Davy shook the man's hand. He opened the door to his room so they could enter.

"What's on your minds?" he asked.

"Well, Davy, you have done a fine job here in the state legislature. But we think you could do an even better job for us in Washington. We want you to run for the United States Congress."

Davy sat in silence. The children watched him as he thought about the man's request.

"The United States Congress. That is quite a step up. I don't know if enough folks know me to get elected to that position."

The men smiled. "Don't worry, Davy. Lots of folks know who you are. You'd be surprised how popular you are in this state. And you know Andrew Jackson, the President. You were in the Indian wars with him. That would be a big help in getting laws passed to help our area."

The children saw a smile slowly cross Davy's face.

"I believe that you are right. I think I will have a go at this Congress business. When do we start?"

The men all smiled and slapped Davy on the back. "We'll get started right away. There is a debate tomorrow. Your opponent has heard that we wanted you to run. He is writing a speech just to make fun of you."

Davy looked at the children. "That so? Well, we might have some fun with him ourselves."

The next day, a large crowd had gathered to hear the candidates speak. Davy's opponent was a wealthy landowner from the eastern part of the state. He spoke first.

"My fellow Tennesseans. You have the opportunity to select a man to represent you in Congress who can do great things for this state and for you. I know many influential men who could use their influence, at my request, to help us move forward." His speech was interrupted by a flock of guinea hens that flew in front of him making a loud noise. When the guinea hens had left he continued. "My opponent cannot offer you this. He is nothing but a 'gentleman' from the cane. We all know what these canebrake folks are like. They do not have the intelligence, the education, or the ability to lead us where we need to go. That's why I am asking you to vote for me for Congress. Together we can move this state forward to a new era of great growth and wealth. Thank you."

He bowed to Davy as he sat down. Davy sat looking at the crowd for several moments. Then he rose and slowly walked to the center of the stage. He smiled out at the crowd.

"Well, after listening to my opponent, I guess I'm just wasting my time and yours by being here. Yes, I am from the canebrake. But so are most of you. I found that there are some nice, hard-working folks living in the canebrake. People who are not afraid to get their hands dirty doing an honest day's work. People who are willing to help out a neighbor when he needs it. Shoot, I guess I don't know any better than to be proud that I'm from the canebrake. I know this, I don't know many rich folks like this fellow here does, but I know many of you, and if you elect me then I promise you I will do all I can to see that you get what you need. When that flock of guinea hens interrupted my opponent, I was trying to make out what they were saying. I finally figured it out. They were saying 'Crockett! Crockett! Crockett!' I would greatly appreciate your vote."

The crowd cheered and laughed as Davy sat down. The man who asked him to run for Congress leaned over and whispered in his ear.

"You better get ready to move to Washington, Congressman Crockett."

# Chapter Eight

Davy looked around the small room where he would be staying in Washington. He had won the election and had come to the nation's capital to begin his career as a congressman from Tennessee. The children watched him as he unpacked his few belongings.

"Well, Davy," Braden said. "How do you feel now that you're a member of Congress?"

Davy sat down on the bed. "I guess I don't feel much different. I feel more responsibility for the folks back home. I need to make sure I represent them well. But, you know I have always lived by the motto, 'be always sure you are right, then go ahead'. I think if I live up to that, then everything will be all right."

Addie looked out the window. "Washington sure is a busy place. People are everywhere."

Dylan stood by her side. "Yes. They look like a bunch of ants, scurrying every which way. It sure is different from the forests of Tennessee."

Davy nodded his head. "Sure is. I guess it will take some getting used to."

Someone knocked at the door, and Davy opened it. A small man in a fancy suit was standing at the door.

"Congressman Crockett? I am Silas Cooper. I am a secretary for President Jackson. He requests that you stop by for a visit today. Would three o'clock be all right?"

Davy looked at the small man standing there. "President Jackson wants to see me? Well then, I suppose I should go meet the President. Mr. Cooper, tell President Jackson that I would be honored to meet with him at three o'clock."

Silas Cooper bowed and backed out of the door. "I shall, Congressman Crockett." He turned and walked down the hall.

Davy shut the door and walked back into the room. "I wonder what he wants," he said. "I haven't seen General...I mean President Jackson, since the Indian wars."

"Maybe he just wants to talk about old times," Braden said.

Davy nodded. "Could be. I don't remember him as being someone who just sits down and visits without wanting something. I guess we will find out shortly."

At three o'clock, Silas Cooper led Davy into a large office. The three children followed. President Jackson was sitting behind a large desk signing some papers. He looked up as Davy walked in. The President smiled and rose from his chair. He walked around the desk and shook Davy's hand.

"It's good to see you again, Congressman Crockett."

"It's good to see you too, Mr. President."

President Jackson motioned to a chair. "Have a seat, Davy. I think I will call you Davy instead of Congressman Crockett, if you don't mind."

Davy sat in the chair. "I don't mind at all, Mr. President."

President Jackson sat down behind his desk and lit a cigar. He offered one to Davy, but he declined.

"Now, Davy. You are probably wondering why I asked to meet with you."

"The thought had crossed my mind," Davy said.

# David Crockett

The President blew a cloud of smoke toward the ceiling. "Davy, this term of Congress is going to be very important for our country. Some important bills are going to be introduced. I am hoping that I can count on your support for my programs in the coming session."

Davy thought for a minute before he spoke. "Mr. President, I sure hope we can work together in this Congress. But I was elected by the voters of my district in Tennessee to represent them in Congress. I have to vote for what's best for them."

"Certainly, Davy. I understand that. But I think you will see that my programs are what are best for the people back home. Don't forget, I'm from Tennessee too. There are sure some good folks back there. I look forward to the day that I can move back home and be with them again."

"I feel the same way, Mr. President."

President Jackson rose and walked over to Davy. "Thank you for stopping by. I know you have many things to do. We will talk again."

Davy stood up. "It was nice to see you again, Mr. President. I look forward to our next visit."

Davy walked out of the room. The children followed him. President Jackson watched him go then turned to Silas Cooper, who was standing next to him. "Well, Silas. I'm afraid we are dealing with an honest man. I don't think that Congressman Crockett will blindly follow where I want to lead him. We will need to keep an eye on him."

Out in the hall, Addie and the others walked with Davy. "Davy, what did you think of the President?" she asked.

Davy took a deep breath. "I am afraid that the President and I are going to have some disagreements about what's best for the people of Tennessee. I hope not. But if it comes to that, I will have to make sure I am right, then go ahead."

# Chapter Nine

ADDIE, DYLAN, AND BRADEN SAT IN THE GALLERY and watched as Davy walked out onto the floor of the Congress. Several members of Congress walked over and shook his hand. Davy was shown to his desk and took a seat. Soon the Speaker of the House pounded his gavel and called the meeting to order.

"Gentlemen of the Congress of the United States," he said. "We have some new members with us today. At this time I am going to call on each one to introduce himself and tell us something about him."

The speaker called out the names of several

men. Each would rise when his name was called and then sit down to polite applause. Finally the Speaker called out Davy's name. Davy rose from his seat. He looked uncomfortable in his new suit with the starched white collar. He looked around the room then began to speak.

"Howdy. My name is David Crockett. I am from Tennessee. I am not used to being in a building this nice. I am more comfortable being in the woods. There all you have to watch out for is bears and Indians. Looking around here, I'm not too sure what I should watch out for."

The members laughed at Davy's joke. He smiled then continued.

"When I was elected to this office, I promised the folks back home that I would represent them the best I could in this Congress. I mean to do that. I feel that I have been given a high honor by being elected to this Congress. I want to make the voters back home glad they elected me."

Davy sat down as the other members of Congress applauded. When all the new members of Congress had been introduced, the day's business began. The children were soon bored and walked outside. They walked around the building watching the people pass by. Everyone seemed to be in a hurry. Finally the friends sat in the shade of a tree and waited for Davy to come out of the building.

"We are going to have the best paper in the class," Dylan said.

"We sure are," Braden agreed. "I can't wait to start writing it."

Addie looked up at a bird sitting on a branch of the tree. "We still have to get more information. Then we have to figure out how to get back home. I don't really know where you find that light we walked through to get here."

Dylan stretched out on the grass. "Oh, I imagine that Davy will show us how to get home."

"Sure," Braden agreed. "I am not worried as long as Davy is around."

Soon the doors to the building opened and Davy walked out. The children noticed that he had a worried look on his face.

"What's wrong, Davy?" Addie asked.

Davy sat down next to the three children.

"I am not sure I like the way that Congress works."

"What do you mean, Davy?" asked Braden.

Davy took a deep breath and leaned against the tree. "It seems to me that those men in there are not interested in what is best for the folks that elected them. They are more interested in what is good for them. I don't think I can work with people like that. I think the folks that elected me are who I should look after. If I can't do what is best for them, I need to go back to the forests and let somebody else take this job."

"What do those men want, Davy?" Braden asked.

"There are some projects that will put some money in the pockets of the men backing them. The thing is, they will raise the taxes of the folks in Tennessee, and they won't get any benefit from the project. They are asking me to support their plan. I don't think I can do it."

"What happens if you don't support them, Davy?" asked Dylan.

"Then they will work to see I don't get reelected. It seems the President is in favor of the project. So if I don't support it, I will be fighting him."

Addie smiled at Davy. "Well, you know what you say. 'Be always sure you're right, then go ahead'. If you are sure you're right not to support the President, then go ahead and not support him."

Davy stood up and brushed the dirt from his clothes. "Thanks. I think you're right. I got to live to make David Crockett happy when he looks in the mirror. If somebody else is not happy then I guess I can't worry about them. Come on. Let's get something to eat. I'm hungry enough to eat a fair-sized skunk."

# Chapter Ten

THE MONTHS PASSED BY and Davy became a well-known member of Congress. The other members of Congress respected him for his honesty. He was friendly, and everyone was glad to see him when he arrived at the Capitol every day. Addie, Dylan, and Braden enjoyed listening to him when he spoke before the other members of Congress. Soon he was being asked to parties and other social gatherings. He was always welcome, but Davy felt uncomfortable at these events. He said he felt more at home in the forest.

One day while Davy and the children were in his

room, they heard a knock on the door. Davy opened the door and saw Silas Cooper standing there.

"Good afternoon, Congressman Crockett," Silas said.

"Good afternoon, Mr. Cooper. What brings you out on such a hot day?"

"The President would like to meet with you this afternoon at two o'clock. If you can make it."

Davy stood in silence for a while. "What does the President want to talk to me about?"

"I don't know, sir. I was just told to bring this message to you."

Davy looked back at the children, who were watching him. "Tell the President that I will be happy to meet with him."

Silas Cooper bowed and walked away. Davy walked over and sat in a chair.

"I have a bad feeling about this meeting. The President has not even said hello since our first visit. He is up to something and wants me to help him."

"Well, Davy," Addie said. "You can always tell him no."

Davy shook his head. "It is not always easy to tell the President of the United States no." He looked at his watch. "I guess I better get ready. A person should look nice when he goes to visit the President."

# David Crockett

Shortly before two o'clock, Silas Cooper opened the door and Davy walked into the President's office. President Jackson looked up from the paper he was reading. When he saw Davy, he rose from his chair and walked over to him. He shook Davy's hand.

"Congressman Crockett. Nice of you to come. Please have a seat. Would you like something to drink?"

"No, thank you, Mr. President."

President Jackson sat down in a chair facing Davy. "Let's cut out the Mr. Presidents and Congressman Crocketts. We've known each other a long time. Fought together. It should be Andy and Davy."

Davy looked at President Jackson. "Whatever you say Mr. ...Andy."

The President leaned forward in his chair. "Davy, you have done well since you have been in Congress. I have watched you with interest. You are the kind of man I want working with me."

"Thank you Mr. President."

"Now, Davy. There is a bill going before Congress soon. This bill is very important to me. I want you to help me get the bill passed."

Davy shifted in his chair. "I don't know how much help I can be, Andy. What kind of bill is it?"

President Jackson rose from his chair and walked

over to the window. He gazed out at the people walking below.

"Davy, all those people walking on the street down there. They're voters. And all those folks moving out to the west, they vote too."

"Yes they do, Andy."

"These people moving west are looking for land. A place to start a new life."

"There's plenty of land out there, Andy."

President Jackson turned to face Davy. "Yes there is, Davy. But the problem is that the land the settlers want is already taken. It seems that some Indian tribes have been living there. This is good land. We can move the Indians to other land. Land that the settlers don't want. What do you say, Davy. Can I count on you?"

Davy stood up. "Mr. President, didn't we make a treaty with these Indians telling them they could have this land?"

President Jackson turned back to the window.

"Yes. A long time ago."

"Far as I know, the Indians have kept their part of the treaty. I think we should keep our part. I promised some of the Indians that I would do what I could to see they did not lose their land. I have tried to keep my promise. It would not be right to move these people from their homes so that someone else can move in.

# David Crockett

There is plenty of land out there. Let the settlers move to that land."

"Congressman Crockett. You don't seem to understand. We need to let these settlers have this land. The Indians can live anywhere."

"I think I do understand, Mr. President. I wonder if you would be for moving these Indians off the land if they could vote."

The President turned to Davy. His face was red with anger. "You need to understand this. If you don't work with me, it could be very hard for you to be reelected."

Davy picked up his hat. "I know one thing, Mr. President. When I look in the mirror every morning when I shave, I need to like the fellow who is looking back at me. I don't think I would like the man very much who ran the Indians off their land for no reason."

"Think about it, Congressman Crockett. Think very hard about it. Good day."

"Good day, Mr. President."

Davy turned and walked out of the room. The children ran after him. When they were outside, Dylan looked at Davy.

"What are you going to do, Davy? If you don't do what the President wants, he could see that you are defeated in the next election."

# Robert E. Hollmann

Davy kept walking.

"There are some things more important than being reelected. I hope I never get to the point that I will throw away all I believe in to get someone's vote. Well, here we are. Home again."

They walked up the stairs to Davy's room. Two men were waiting outside the room. They smiled when they saw Davy walk up.

One of them walked over and shook Davy's hand. "Congressman Crockett. Good to see you. We are members of the Whig Party. We would like to invite you to come to Philadelphia and speak to our group."

Davy looked at the two men. "What do you want me to speak about?"

"Why, just tell us your story. We hear you are a most interesting fellow. There are many people in Philadelphia who want a chance to meet you and shake your hand. Will you come?"

Davy looked at the children. "Why, I would be most honored." He turned to his three friends. "Well, kids. What do you say we go see what things are like in Philadelphia?"

Braden looked at the two men. "Sure, Davy. I guess that things couldn't be worse than in Washington."

# Chapter
# Eleven

ADDIE, DYLAN, AND BRADEN LOOKED AROUND the streets of Philadelphia. The sidewalks were crowded as people rushed about. Davy talked to the men from the Whig party as they led him to a theater.

"I believe you will enjoy this show, Congressman Crockett," one of the men said.

His friend nodded. "Yes. This show is put on for you."

Davy smiled. "I look forward to seeing it."

Soon they stood in front of a theater. A long line of people were waiting to get inside.

The children looked at a poster hanging on the wall. Addie read the poster.

"Nimrod Wildfire is the Lion of the West." She looked at the picture painted on the poster. "That looks like you, Davy."

Davy stared at the poster. "Yes it does." He turned to the men who were watching him. "What is this show about?"

One of the men laughed. "Why, Congressman Crockett, it's about you. Come on, let's go inside."

They walked into the theater and sat in a box next to the stage. Soon the curtain opened and a man in buckskins and a coonskin cap walked out on stage. He bowed toward Davy. Davy nodded back at him. The actor turned back to the audience.

"Good evening, ladies and gentlemen. My name is Nimrod Wildfire. I am half horse, half alligator, and a little part of a snapping turtle. I eat lightning and blink thunder. I can run faster, jump higher, dive deeper and come up dryer than any man alive. I got the fastest horse, the prettiest wife, and the ugliest dog in the world. I welcome you here tonight to share my adventures in the wilds of the American wilderness. But, before we begin our journey, I want to introduce a very special guest tonight. We are honored to have with us the reallife Lion of the West, The Honorable David Crockett from

Tennessee."

The crowd applauded, and Davy stood and waved to them. After a while the applause stopped and Davy motioned for the show to go on. When the show was over, Davy and his friends walked outside. One of the men with them took Davy by the arm and led him down the street.

"Congressman, we would like for you to come with us. Our party is having a dinner in your honor."

Soon Davy was sitting at the head table. Addie, Dylan, and Braden stood to one side and watched. After the meal a man stood and banged on a glass with a spoon. The room went silent as the man began to speak.

"Gentlemen. We are honored to have with us tonight the Honorable Congressman from Tennessee, David Crockett."

Davy stood as the men in the room clapped. He raised his hand and the room became silent.

"Thank you, gentlemen. I want to thank you for a very nice evening. The show was good and the dinner was mighty fine. I have not met so many good men since I left Tennessee. I wish your party well in the coming elections. From what I have seen in Washington, we could use new leadership, and I think you can provide it. I will do what I can to help you. Together we can put the country back on the right path."

The men clapped again as Davy sat down. The man sitting next to him stood up and raised his hand.

"Congressman Crockett, the Whig Party of Philadelphia has a gift for you." He pulled a rifle from under the table. "We would like to present this rifle to you as a token of our respect for you."

Davy stood and took the rifle. He looked at the barrel. On the end of the barrel were the words "Go Ahead." He lifted the rifle and turned to the crowd of men who were now standing.

"Thank you very much. I appreciate this gift very much. You know, this rifle is so pretty that I think it should have a name. I think I will call it Betsy. And I tell you, I will keep her with me all the time. Thank you again."

The men clapped again as Davy sat back down. The children smiled as they watched Davy shake hands with all the men in the room. Braden turned to Addie and Dylan.

"You know, I think Davy is going to need that rifle when the President hears about this."

# Chapter
# Twelve

THE LARGE ROOM WAS UNUSUALLY QUIET. Members of Congress stood in small groups and whispered among themselves. Several of them looked up as the door opened and Davy walked to his desk. A few of the men nodded, but no one spoke to him. Davy sat down and looked at some papers. Addie, Dylan, and Braden sat in the balcony watching the men on the floor of the room. The Speaker of the House stood and pounded on his desk with a large gavel. The men sat at their desks and listened to the Speaker.

"Gentlemen. We have before us today a bill

that is favored by the President. It is a bill that calls for the removal of certain Indian tribes from certain lands and moving them to other lands where they can make their homes. We will now open this matter to any discussion."

Several members of Congress stood and spoke in favor of the bill. They were all friends of President Jackson. They hoped that by supporting the bill, they would receive support from the President in their upcoming elections. When all who supported the bill had spoken, the Speaker asked if anyone wished to talk against the bill. The men all looked around the room. Some members shuffled in their seats, but no one got up. Finally Davy rose slowly from his chair. The children listened as he spoke.

"I would like to say something about this," he said. All the members of Congress watched him as he began to speak.

"I have not been a member of this Congress for as long as some of you. Since I have been here, I have watched with great interest the way that things are done. I have not always agreed with the way some bills were passed, but I accepted the fact that things work differently here than they do back home. But I cannot sit here and watch this bill get passed into law without speaking out for those who cannot speak for themselves."

# David Crockett

Davy walked around in front of his desk. All eyes were on him.

"When I came here, I told the folks back home that I would do my best to represent them. I have tried to do that. I also told a tribe of Indians that I would do everything I could to help them keep their lands and their homes. I intend to do that. I gave them my word, and I gave them my hand. To me that is the most sacred thing a man can give. If a man's word is no good, then the man is no good. The government of the United States gave its word to these same Indians. Now it wants to break its word to them. You must be able to trust the word of the government, just like you must be able to trust the word of a man. I say we must make the word of the government good and not pass this bill. We must not move these people from their homes. It is true that they cannot vote. But that does not mean they do not have rights as people. They have the right to live peacefully in their homes. For the government to break that peace is wrong. For you to vote to pass this bill is wrong. I ask you to do the right thing and vote to defeat this bill. If you do, you will feel a lot better about the man staring back at you in the mirror."

Davy sat down. There was not a sound in the room. Finally the Speaker stood and called for a vote. Some members of Congress voted with Davy against the bill. However, most of the men voted for it, and the bill passed. Davy walked outside and found Addie, Dylan, and Braden waiting for him.

"What are you going to do now, Davy?" Braden asked.

Davy put his hand on Braden's shoulder. "I am going home. I have to win an election."

Several months later Davy and his friends sat in Davy's cabin and listened to the sound of people cheering outside. The election was over, and Davy had lost. Dylan looked across the table at Davy.

"I am sorry you lost, Davy," he said.

Davy smiled. "Well, that's all right. To tell you the truth, I was getting tired of Washington. I never felt like I fit in there. I think it is time I moved on."

"Where you moving to, Davy?" Addie asked.

"I have heard of this place where the hunting is good and the land is there for anyone who wants it. The climate is nice and the people are friendly. I think I will go check it out. Yes, I think I will go to Texas."

# Chapter
# Thirteen

THE GRASS REACHED TO THE BELLIES OF THE HORSES as the small group of riders rode along. Davy was in front, followed by a few of his friends who had joined him for his trip to Texas. Addie, Dylan, and Braden rode in back of the others. It seemed to them that they had been riding forever. They had enjoyed the riverboat ride down the Mississippi River, but since they had crossed into Texas it seemed to them that the land never ended.

"I never realized how big Texas was," Addie said.

Dylan stood up in his stirrups. "I never realized

how hard a horse was. I won't complain about riding in a car again."

The day was warm, and the rhythm of the horses almost rocked the riders to sleep. Suddenly the ground began to shake. A loud rumble could be heard. A large cloud of dust appeared on the horizon. Soon a large brown mass came into view.

"What is that?" Braden asked.

Davy and his friends studied the oncoming mass. Suddenly Davy waved his cap and shouted.

"It's buffalo. Come on. Let's get some dinner for tonight."

The men raced after the fast-moving herd. The three friends rode as fast as they could, but could not keep up with Davy. Soon the herd and the riders disappeared over a small hill. Addie and the others hurried to catch up. They heard some popping noises. The children realized that the men were shooting at the buffalo. They came to the top of the small hill and saw the last of the herd disappearing from sight. Davy and his friends were standing next to a buffalo. The children rode up to him.

"We will eat good tonight. There is nothing better than roast buffalo. That was the biggest herd I have ever seen. It seems that the stories about Texas are true. There is good hunting and plenty of land. It is getting

# David Crockett

late. Let's set up camp here."

Soon the men had the camp set up. The smell of roasting buffalo filled the air. It made the children hungry to smell the meat cooking. As they were waiting for the meat to cook, several men rode up to the camp. Davy stood and went to greet them.

"Howdy. My name's Davy Crockett. Get down and rest. We will have dinner ready soon. You're welcome to eat with us."

The leader of the men shook his head. "Thank you. But we need to keep moving. We have a ways to go, and we are in a hurry."

Davy walked over to the man. "Where are you going in such a hurry?"

"We are on our way to San Antonio. The Texas army is there. They are waiting for Santa Anna, the President of Mexico. They need more men."

"This Santa Anna going to cause trouble?"

The man nodded. "He is bringing his army. The people of Texas want to be independent, but Santa Anna wants to keep us part of Mexico. There are not very many men there now. That is why we are in such a hurry. It is important that we stop Santa Anna before he gets to the settlements."

Davy looked in the direction the men were traveling. "Where is San Antonio?"

"It's a couple of days' journey to the west. I am sure that the men there would be glad to have you join them."

Davy shook his head. "Thank you, but we are just looking around. I hope you have a safe trip."

The men waved to Davy and his friends and rode away. They watched the men ride off. One of Davy's friends turned to him.

"What do you think about that, Davy? Looks like we might be riding into a big fight."

Davy shook his head. "I don't think so. San Antonio is a long way from here. We can just go on exploring and never come anywhere near the fight. Well, it looks like the meat is done. Let's eat."

That night Addie lay on her blanket looking up at the stars. She couldn't remember them being so bright back in Eden Prairie. The moon was full, and Addie could see the horses clearly as they grazed on the tall grass. Davy was lying beside her. She could tell he was not asleep.

"Davy, what do you think about Texas so far?"

"Why, it is just about the prettiest place I have ever seen. I think it will make a good place to start a home."

"What about the war?"

She could hear Davy sigh. "Well, Addie, I have

been thinking about that. Sometimes it seems that if you want something, you might have to fight to keep others from taking it away from you. From what I have seen, Texas would be worth fighting for."

"So you are thinking about going to San Antonio?"

"We will just keep riding and see where we end up. Now you better get some sleep. Tomorrow will be another long day."

# Chapter
# Fourteen

THE DAYS PASSED, and the group of riders saw a lot of pretty countryside. Yellow flowers covered the prairie like a carpet. Sometimes blue or red flowers joined the yellow ones to make the landscape look like a picture. The tall grass provided plenty of food for the horses, and the men were able to provide their food from the different types of game that roamed the plains.

The children enjoyed seeing Texas in this new way. Dylan shifted in his saddle and said, "I never realized how pretty the country could be. When you are driving seventy miles an hour down a paved road, it all looks different."

# David Crockett

"Sure does," Braden agreed. "I wonder where Davy is going?"

"I don't know," Addie said. "We have been following this road for a couple of days. Some of the men said it goes to San Antonio."

Dylan looked at Addie. "San Antonio. That's where the enemy army is heading. I thought Davy didn't want to go there."

"I don't know," Addie said as she looked at a covey of quail that flew from the grass. "I am just guessing. If Davy thinks it is right to fight for Texas, then he will."

Davy was riding in front of the group. He pulled his horse to a stop and looked at a small cabin nestled in a group of trees. Smoke was coming from the cabin, and several children were playing in front of it. Davy and the others rode up to the children and pulled their horses to a stop.

Davy smiled down at the oldest boy. "Howdy. My name's David Crockett. I'm from Tennessee. My friends and I are exploring Texas. I wonder if your folks are at home so I could visit with them."

The boy looked up at Davy. He glanced at the other men. "My pa's gone. My ma's here. Wait and I will go get her."

The boy disappeared into the house. Shortly he

came back leading a woman by the hand. He stopped in front of Davy.

"Ma, this is Mr. Crockett from Tennessee. He and his friends are exploring the country. He wants to talk to you." The woman stared straight ahead. As Davy looked at her he realized that she was blind. He got down from his horse and walked to her.

"Howdy, ma'am. David Crockett. These are my friends. I was wanting to ask some questions about the country around here."

The woman held out her hand. "I have heard of you. Mr. Crockett. Have you by chance seen my husband? His name is Isaac Millsaps. He left some time ago to go to San Antonio."

Davy shook his head. "No, ma'am. I haven't seen your husband. But we haven't been to San Antonio. We have come from the East."

Mrs. Millsaps smiled. "I will be happy to talk to you. I don't know that I can be of any help. Won't you and your friends get down and join us for supper? I am sure we can put something together for you."

"We would enjoy eating with you. Don't worry about food. Hunting has been good. Texas is loaded with game. We have plenty of meat to share with you and your family."

After supper, Davy and Mrs. Millsaps sat outside

the cabin. The children sat nearby listening. Davy looked at the clear, star-filled sky.

"You said your husband went to San Antonio, did he go to join the army there?"

"Yes. He and several neighbors went together. A messenger came through one day saying the army needed men. Isaac and the others felt they should go do their part to protect our home. The night before he left, we sat right here and talked. We talked about the old days in Mississippi. We talked about how much we liked it in Texas. We have made a new start here. It is our home now."

"Yes, ma'am. From what I have seen, Texas is a real pretty place. A nice place to make a home."

"Isaac and me used to sit out here and he would describe the country. The flowers, the wildlife, and the sunsets. I wish I could see them, but when he described them to me, it was like I could see them, and they were beautiful. Mr. Crockett, if you do happen to see my husband, would you give him a message from me?"

"Why I would be happy to, ma'am."

"Tell him that we love him and we miss him and we hope he hurries home."

"I surely will. I imagine he wants to get home as fast as he can."

Mrs. Millsaps stood up. "I better go in and get the

children ready for bed."

Davy watched as she walked inside the cabin. He sat there staring at the ground in silence. Finally Addie sat next to him. "What are you thinking about, Davy?"

Davy looked at her and the other children. "I am thinking we better get some sleep. We have an early start and a long ride tomorrow."

"Where are we going?" Dylan asked.

Davy stood up and stretched. "San Antonio. We have a message to deliver."

# Chapter
# Fifteen

"THERE SHE IS, DAVY. SAN ANTONIO." One of Davy's companions pointed to the buildings rising from the plains. "Looks good, doesn't it?"

"Sure does" Davy took off his cap and looked at the buildings. "Guess we should ride down and say hello."

The children followed the men as they rode into the town. The dusty street was crowded with people. Adobe buildings lined the street. The interiors of the buildings looked dark and cool. Davy stopped his horse in front of a blacksmith shop. A strong-looking man was pounding on a horseshoe.

Davy dismounted and walked over to the blacksmith. "Howdy. My name's David Crockett. My friends and I have just arrived from Tennessee."

The blacksmith wiped his hands on his leather apron and shook Davy's hand.

"Glad to meet you. My name's Almeron Dickinson. I'm from Tennessee myself. Iheard of you, Mr. Crockett. Glad to meet you."

"Call me David. Or Davy if you heard the stories. What's going on here, Almeron?"

"Everybody's getting ready for Santa Anna and his army. They should be here anytime. Colonel Travis doesn't think they will be here for sevral weeks, but we have had reports that they are getting close."

"Colonel Travis. He the one in charge?"

"Yes. Well, he and Bowie are splitting the command right now. Trouble is, they don't always agree. Bowie believes the reports that Santa Anna is near. He wants us to get ready faster. Not a good situation to have your leaders fighting when an enemy army is coming."

"Where would I find these two?" Davy asked.

Almeron Dickinson pointed across the street. "That's Travis's office. I don't know where Bowie is."

The back door of the shop opened, and a young woman walked in carrying a baby.

# David Crockett

"Davy, this is my wife, Susannah. And my daughter, Angelina. Susannah, this is the famous Davy Crockett. You remember we heard about him back in Tennessee."

The young lady extended her hand. "Of course I remember. Nice to meet you, Mr. Crockett."

Davy took her hand. "Please, ma'am, call me Davy. It makes feel old to be called Mr. Crockett."

Davy smiled down at the baby.

"You have a lovely daughter, Susannah. Well, I guess I better go meet Colonel Travis. I hope to see you later."

Davy and his friends walked across the street. Addie, Dylan, and Braden followed Davy into the small room. A young man was sitting at a small desk writing a letter. He looked up as Davy entered.

"Yes, sir. What can I do for you?"

Davy walked over to the desk.

"Colonel Travis? My name is David Crockett. I hear you are in charge here."

Travis stood up. "Congressman Crockett. It is a great pleasure to meet you."

"Please, don't call me Congressman. Those days are long gone. Call me David, or Davy."

Travis motioned to a chair. "Please sit down, Davy. I am glad you are here."

Davy sat in the chair. Addie and the others stood behind him.

"Colonel Travis, I hear that Santa Anna is getting close."

Travis laughed. "Those are rumors being spread by people who are scared by their own shadows. This is February, Davy. The grass is dead. Where would Santa Anna get food for his animals? He will need a lot of animals to transport such a large army. No, I believe he will wait until spring, when the grass is green."

"I don't know, Colonel. My friends and I just crossed the plains to get here. That dry grass made good food for our horses. They ate it like it was good anyway."

Travis turned in his chair. He did not like to have his ideas questioned.

"Trust me, Davy. I have been here longer than you. I know an army cannot cross this country in the winter."

"Well, if you say so. On the way here we stopped at Isaac Millsaps's place. His wife wanted me to give him a message. Do you happen to know where he is?"

Travis thought for a moment. "I believe he is with Green Jameson working on the defenses of the Alamo." Davy stood up. "It was nice to meet you. I think I will go over to the Alamo and try to find Mr. Millsaps."

Travis walked him to the door. "I will talk to you later, Davy. I would like to talk to you about the upcoming battle."

Davy walked outside the office. He walked over to his friends who had been waiting for him. One of the men walked over to him.

"Well, Davy. What are we going to do?"

Davy looked back at Travis's office and then toward the old mission on the outskirts of town.

"Well, I guess we are going to the Alamo."

# Chapter Sixteen

THE ALAMO BUZZED WITH ACTIVITY as Davy and his friends rode through the gates of the old mission. A group of men were placing cannons on the walls. Another group was digging a well in the center of the courtyard. A third group was building a wooden fence on the south part of the Alamo to close a gap in the walls. Davy dismounted and walked over to a group of men who were pushing a cannon up a ramp to the top of the Alamo chapel.

"Howdy. I am David Crockett. I am looking for Isaac Millsaps."

A man walked over to him. "I am Green Jameson.

I am in charge of building the defenses here. I think Isaac is here somewhere. Gregorio, do you know where Isaac is?"

A man who was pushing the cannon up the ramp stopped and wiped his head with a handkerchief. "I think he and Antonio Fuentes were working on the North wall." The man extended his hand to Davy. "I am Gregorio Esparza. It is nice to meet you."

"Nice to meet you too. I think I will take a walk to the north wall."

Davy walked through the Alamo courtyard. He passed the men digging the well. They were taking a break and watched Davy as he walked past. Davy found some men working on the north wall. He walked up to the group.

"Howdy. Would one of you happen to be Isaac Millsaps?"

One man walked over to Davy.

"That would be me. Who are you?"

"My name is David Crockett. We stopped by your place on the way here, and your wife asked me to look you up."

"How is my family doing?"

"Your wife is doing fine. So are the children. All seven of them."

Millsaps smiled. "That makes me feel better. I

sure hated to go and leave them."

"She said they miss you and hope you can get home soon."

Millsaps smiled. "If Colonel Travis is right, Santa Anna won't be here for several weeks. When I get through here, I might go home for a while."

Davy turned to go. "I guess I better find a place for my men and me to stay. I hope to see you later."

Davy walked back across the courtyard.

"Davy Crockett."

Davy turned and saw a big man walking toward him.

"Glad to see you. My name is Jim Bowie. This is my good friend, Juan Seguin."

Davy shook his hand. "Good to meet you. I have heard a lot about you. And your knife."

Bowie laughed. "I think more people know about my knife than about me."

"I met Colonel Travis in town. I understand that you and he share the command."

Bowie shook his head. "I don't think Travis likes that arrangement. He wants to be in charge." Bowie coughed. He doubled over with pain, then stood back up and smiled weakly at Davy.

"Dadgum cough. I don't know what's wrong. A bad cold, I guess."

# David Crockett

"That sounds like more than a cold," Davy said. "Have you seen a doctor?"

Bowie nodded. "I have seen several. They don't really know what is wrong. I think it will be better when the weather warms up."

Davy looked over at his friends, who were watching him. "Do you know where we might find a place to stay in town?"

Bowie wiped some sweat from his face. "There aren't too many places to stay in town. I have several empty rooms in my house. You and your men are welcome to stay there until something better becomes available."

Davy smiled at Bowie. "Thank you, Jim. I think I will take you up on your offer."

Bowie turned to his friend. "Juan, will you show Davy and his friends to my house? I need to meet with Travis."

"Sure, Jim. If you and your friends will come with me, Davy."

Davy walked away with Juan. He turned to Bowie. "I will see you later, Jim."

Bowie waved then coughed again.

"What is really wrong with him, Juan?"

Juan shook his head. "I don't know. But I think it is very serious. I do know that we cannot afford to lose him as a commander of the Alamo. The men respect him. I don't know if Travis can lead them."

Davy looked at the old mission as he walked with Juan. The walls were thick, but there were no loopholes to fire through. Some parapets had been built, but anyone firing from them would be exposed to enemy fire. It was not a place that gave Davy much hope that it could be successfully defended.

Juan turned to Davy. "Let's get you and your men settled in. There is a party tonight."

"What is the party for?" Davy asked.

"George Washington's birthday. It should be a nice party. With Santa Anna on the way, there is no telling when the next party will be."

# Chapter
# Seventeen

THE SOUNDS OF FIDDLES AND GUITARS FILLED THE NIGHT AIR. Addie, Dylan, and Braden stood under a tree and watched the couples dancing on the dusty street. Young women from town joined the Alamo defenders for the party. Stern faced chaperones watched the dancers. They were ready to intervene if the dancing became too close.

"I don't think I have ever seen dancing like that," Braden said.

Dylan shook his head. "No. It sure is different from the dances we see in Eden Prairie. Looks like they are having fun, though."

"Looks to me like they are stomping on snakes. I wonder what Davy and Colonel Travis are talking about?" Addie said.

Davy and Colonel Travis sat at a small table. They ignored the dancers as they talked about Santa Anna's approaching army.

"I think you should pay more attention to the stories that Santa Anna is on his way," Davy said. "These people are taking a chance to warn you about his army."

"I know that, Davy. But it makes no sense that he could move an army that large across the desert of Northern Mexico in the winter. These people are scared, and they are seeing things that are not there. By the time Santa Anna gets here, we will have received many reinforcements, and we will be able to stop him right here."

"Do you really think that old mission can stand up to a real fight? When I was there today, it looked like it was ready to fall down."

Travis shook his head. "I know there is much to be done, but Green Jameson and the others are doing the best they can. You should have seen it before they began working on it. They have made a lot of improvements."

"I don't mean to criticize their work. I just do

not like to be hemmed in. I would rather fight in the open."

Travis looked at the dancers. "You sound like Bowie. He wants to move on and fight them in the open too. But if we leave San Antonio, we give the enemy one of the major cities in Texas. They can use it for supplies and as a base to move deeper into our settlements. We must stop them here."

The watching children turned as Jim Bowie and a group of men walked up to Davy and Travis. Addie and the others walked closer so they could hear what was being said. Bowie stood in front of Travis.

"This man just rode in. He is one of Juan Seguin's scouts. He said he saw the enemy army not over two days' march away from here. We need to get ready. I still think we need to move out on the plains and fight them in the open."

The children watched Travis as he listened to Bowie. They could tell by his expression that he did not believe the report.

"Colonel Bowie. We receive these reports all the time. According to these people, Santa Anna has done an impossible task. He cannot bring an army that size from Mexico at this time of year."

Juan Seguin frowned when he heard Travis's words. "My men do not lie, Colonel Travis. He is reporting what he saw. He risked his life to bring this news to you."

"I am not saying that he is lying, Juan. I know your men are loyal, and they are doing a great service to our fight for independence. I just think he is mistaken."

Davy looked at the man who had brought the report. "Colonel Travis, I think we should check out this man's story. I will take some men and scout the countryside to see if the enemy army is near."

Travis rose from the table. "I do not have enough men to spare to send on a wild goose chase. If you will excuse me, gentlemen, I will go to my office. I have some reports to write. If it will make you feel better, Colonel Bowie, I will put a man in the bell tower of the church in the morning to watch for signs of the enemy's approach. Good night."

"Why is he so stubborn?" Dylan asked.

Braden watched Travis walk away. "I don't know. He just won't listen to anybody."

Bowie sat down by Davy as Juan and the messenger walked away. "There goes a stubborn man. I think he is going to get us all in a lot of trouble real soon."

Davy shrugged his shoulders. "He is doing what he thinks is right."

"By the way, Davy. I sent Isaac Millsaps home

today. He needs to look after his family."

"That was good of you, Jim. As badly as we need men here, his family needs him more. Well, let's see what is going on at the party."

Several miles away, the army of Santa Anna was camped for the night. Santa Anna was meeting with his officers.

"I have information that the Texans are having a party tonight to honor George Washington. I think it will be easy to surprise them. General Sesma, I want you to take your cavalry and attack that party. If you have trouble, fall back and we will join you in the morning, and together we will destroy the Texans. I want all Texans to understand that if they want to fight me, I will destroy them."

# Chapter
# Eighteen

THE STREETS OF SAN ANTONIO WERE NEARLY EMPTY as Addie, Dylan, and Braden passed by the bell tower. The party had lasted late into the night, and most people were still sleeping. The sentry in the bell tower rubbed his eyes and stared into the distance. Nothing was moving on the flat prairie. He wished that he were still in bed instead of standing in the tower staring at nothing.

"What do you think about the message last night?" Braden asked.

"Davy and Jim Bowie think that it should be taken seriously," Addie said. "I think Colonel Travis does too, or else he would not have put the sentry in the tower."

Dylan pointed down the street. "Here comes Davy and Jim Bowie."

The children watched as the two men walked toward where they were standing. They were having a serious conversation. As they got nearer the children heard Bowie speaking.

"Putting a sentry in the tower is not enough. We should have patrols out searching for Santa Anna's army. I don't care what Travis thinks, I believe that messenger."

Davy looked down the nearly deserted street. "Well, Jim. I guess nothing is keeping us from taking a morning ride."

Just then the bells in the tower began to ring. Everyone looked up and saw the sentry pulling on the bell rope. Colonel Travis ran by and climbed the stairs to the tower. Davy and Jim Bowie followed him. When they reached the top, the sentry pointed and said, "The enemy are in view. They are right over there."

Davy and the others looked where the man was pointing. Nothing moved on the prairie.

"Where is the enemy?" Travis asked.

"Right there," the man answered. He looked and saw that there was nothing on the prairie. "I tell you, I saw a troop of enemy soldiers right there."

Everyone looked again. People were gathering at the bottom of the tower. Someone called up to ask what was going on.

"The sentry thought he saw some enemy troops," Travis called down.

The men on the ground looked where the sentry had pointed. They could see nothing.

"He must have been asleep and dreamed he saw the enemy," someone said.

The people laughed then started back to their homes to go back to sleep.

The sentry was mad that no one believed him. "I tell you, I saw the enemy army. Right over there."

"I think we should check it out," Davy said.

Bowie nodded. "I agree. Davy and I will ride out and see what is there." As he finished speaking, Bowie coughed so hard that he doubled over.

Travis looked at him. "I agree we should check out the report, but you are in no shape to go. Davy is new to the area. I will send some men who know this country." He turned to the sentry. "Stay here. If you see the scouts coming back here at any pace faster than a walk, ring the bell."

Soon two men rode out to check out the place where the sentry said he saw the enemy troops. Davy and Bowie sat at a table in a small café and drank coffee.

"Jim, you need to see a doctor about your cough. It is getting worse."

Bowie waved a hand. "I am all right. It sounds worse than it is."

The children sat nearby, watching the streets begin to fill up with people. Travis came out of his office and walked over to Davy and Bowie.

"Well, so far no news from the scouts. I doubt the sentry saw anything. Sometimes your eyes can play tricks on you. Especially if you are sleepy."

Suddenly the bell in the tower began to ring. Travis, Davy and Bowie rushed up the tower stairs once again. The sentry pointed to where the two scouts had ridden. Davy looked and saw two riders riding toward San Antonio as fast as their horses could run. Travis led the way downstairs and was waiting as the two scouts pulled their horses to a stop.

"What did you see?" Travis asked.

One of the scouts caught his breath and then spoke. "We saw a lot of enemy cavalry. In that dry creek bed, just out of sight. It looks like they are getting ready to attack."

Travis turned to the people standing around him. "The time has come. The enemy is here. Everyone head for the Alamo."

# Chapter
# Nineteen

ADDIE, DYLAN, AND BRADEN WATCHED as the people of San Antonio rushed about the streets. Some of them loaded carts with all their goods and headed out of town. Some grabbed what they could carry and hurried toward the Alamo.

Almeron Dickinson raced his horse down the street and stopped it in front of his house. His wife, Susannah, stood there holding their baby daughter. Dickinson called down to his wife.

"Ask no questions. Give me the baby and climb on behind."

# David Crockett

When Susannah was sitting behind him, he spurred his horse toward the Alamo. The children looked for Davy. They finally found him helping some people load a wagon. He looked up as they approached.

"Hurry and follow me. We must get to the Alamo as soon as possible."

They watched the wagon drive away then followed Davy as he walked toward the old mission. The footbridge over the river was crowded, so they walked downstream and found a shallow place to wade across. Soon they were walking through the gates of the Alamo. Men were working hard to get things ready for the coming battle. Ammunition was carried to the cannons. Some soldiers took their places on the wall and watched for the approach of the enemy army. Gregorio Esparza helped his family get settled in the old chapel then took his place alongside Almeron Dickinson near their cannon.

Travis was in his office writing letters asking for reinforcements. Jim Bowie coughed as he showed men where their places on the wall were. The children jumped out of the way as thirty head of cattle were driven into the courtyard and then into a pen. Several men followed the cattle, carrying bushel baskets of corn. When the last people had entered the mission, the gates were shut and barred.

Davy found his friends standing behind the wooden fence on the south side of the Alamo. He walked over to them.

"What are you doing here?" he asked.

"Travis told us this was our spot. He told us to defend it to the end."

Davy turned and walked toward Travis's room. The children hurried to keep up with him. Davy entered without knocking. Travis looked up from his desk.

"Hello, Davy. I am busy right now. Can we talk later?"

Davy walked over to Travis. "No. We need to talk now. Why did you put us on the weakest part of the defenses? We don't have enough men to hold that spot."

"Davy, you and your men can hold that position better than anybody else I have. We don't have enough men to really defend this mission. That spot is stronger with you and your men there than if I put anybody else. Anyway, I am writing to Colonel Fannin at Goliad and to the legislature, telling them that Santa Anna is here. I am sure that before long we will have many men come to join us, and you will have more men with you."

"You think more men will come here?"

"I am positive. Now excuse me, but I must finish this message. I need to get the messenger on his way before we are cut off."

# David Crockett

Davy walked outside. Men were still rushing to their positions on the wall. He saw a group of defenders, including Bowie, looking toward town. Davy climbed up the wall and stood next to Bowie.

"What are you looking at, Jim?"

Bowie motioned toward the town plaza. A long column of enemy troops was marching into San Antonio. As the defenders watched, a band started to play. Townspeople who had not had a chance to leave lined the streets and watched the troops march past. Bowie pointed to a group of riders wearing bright new uniforms.

"I bet you that is Santa Anna and his staff. Looks like we got out of there just in time." He coughed and leaned against the wall for support.

The children looked on with the others.

"Wow," Dylan said. "Look at that. I have never seen anything like that in my life. There must be thousands of them."

"Yes," Braden said. "They sure make a pretty sight."

"Pretty scary if you ask me," Addie said. "I am starting to wish we had stayed in Eden Prairie."

While the defenders watched, Santa Anna gave a message to one of his officers. The officer grabbed a white flag and rode toward the Alamo. Travis walked up to the group and stood by a cannon. He did not say anything as he watched the enemy officer approach. When the officer was in front of the men on the wall, he stopped his horse. He pulled out a piece of paper and read the message from Santa Anna. The general demanded that the Texans surrender or they would all be killed. The officer asked for the Texan's answer.

Before anyone could say anything, Travis fired the cannon that was next to him. The cannonball skipped harmlessly through town. Travis called down to the enemy officer.

"That is our answer. Tell Santa Anna we shall never surrender or retreat."

# Chapter Twenty

"WHY DID YOU DO THAT?" Bowie screamed at Travis as they sat in Travis's office. "We might have been able to work something out."

Travis yelled back at Bowie. "If you think you can deal with someone like Santa Anna, you are crazier than I think you are."

The children huddled in the corner as the two men yelled at each other. Finally Davy stood between them.

"It doesn't matter now. It has been done. We must get ready to fight Santa Anna, not each other."

Bowie began to cough, and sweat broke out on his forehead. He slumped down into a chair.

"Are you all right, Jim?" Davy asked.

Bowie looked up. His eyes were sunken into his head. "I don't feel very good. I think I better go lie down for a while."

The door opened and Juan Seguin walked in. "The enemy has raised a red flag. It is flying from the tower of San Fernando church."

Travis looked at Bowie. "What does that mean?"

Bowie started to answer, but he began coughing again.

"It means that we can expect no mercy from the enemy. If they win the battle, all of us will be killed," Juan said.

"This is the man you thought we could work a deal with?" Travis said to Bowie. "At least we have some chance if we fight them. Reinforcements will be here soon. I don't know about you, but I will never surrender."

Davy walked over to Bowie. "We can talk about this later. Juan, give me a hand. We need to get Jim to his room. He needs to rest."

Davy and Juan helped Bowie to his feet. As they were walking out the door, Bowie turned to Travis. "I don't know how much good I will be for a while, so I am turning command of the volunteers over to you. I will help all I can."

Travis walked over and put his hand on Bowie's

shoulder. "Thank you, Jim. We must all work together now. I will check on you later."

The children followed Davy and Juan as they helped Bowie across the courtyard. They carried him into his room and laid him on a cot. Bowie was coughing more and his face had turned red. Juan went to get some water while Davy pulled off Bowie's boots.

"I'll talk to some of the ladies about looking after you, Jim." Davy reached into a drawer and pulled out two pistols. "Just in case you need them. I guess you have your Arkansas toothpick handy."

Bowie smiled weakly. He pulled his knife from his belt. "I never let this get too far away."

Davy patted Bowie's shoulder. "I better get back to my post. I will check on you later."

Addie, Dylan, and Braden walked out of the room.

"He looks real sick," Braden said.

Dylan nodded. "It is too bad. He is a real good fighter and I think they are going to need all the fighters they can find."

Davy walked over and sat down by the wooden fence. Addie sat next to him. The boys looked over the fence at the enemy soldiers.

"What do you think, Davy?" she asked.

"I think there is going to be a real big fight here

soon. I hope Travis is right and some people come to help us."

"Are you sorry that you came to Texas?"

Davy smiled. "No. I think Texas is about the prettiest place I have ever seen. A person can make a good life here. I think we are doing what is right. And you know what I say. If you are right, then go ahead."

"Wow. Look at all those soldiers," Dylan said.

Davy and Addie stood up and looked over the fence. A long line of soldiers was marching into the town.

"Well," Davy said. "Looks like Santa Anna got some more men." He looked at the uniforms the soldiers were wearing, and then looked down at his dirty clothes. "At least they look like soldiers."

"Don't worry, Davy," Addie told him. "I know you are a better fighter than any of them."

Davy smiled and shook his head. "Maybe so, but there are sure a lot of them. Oh well. Guess I will take a walk around the fort."

As Davy got up, a cannon fired in the enemy camp. A cannonball hit in the courtyard and exploded. Davy looked at the smoke slowly drifting away from the hole in the ground where the cannonball had exploded. "I guess Santa Anna is showing us he has some cannon too. A whole lot of them."

# Chapter
# Twenty-one

DAVY WALKED INTO THE ALAMO CHAPEL. It took a few minutes for his eyes to adjust to the dim light. The children looked around. The roof had fallen in, and a great pile of rubble was in the middle of the chapel. A ramp had been built to the top of the church, and a cannon sat on top of the ramp. They could hear talking coming from the rooms where the women and children were staying. Susannah Dickinson walked out of one of the rooms. She was carrying her baby. When she saw Davy, she smiled and walked over to him.

"Why, Davy. How nice to see you."

Davy took off his cap. "It is nice to see you too."

Davy looked at the baby. He held out his finger, and the little girl grasped it in her tiny hand.

"Do you like babies, Davy?" Susannah asked.

"Well, I kissed my fair share of them when I was running for Congress. I would have to say I like them much better than most of the politicians I have known."

Susannah walked over and looked at the activity in the Alamo courtyard. Davy stood next to her.

"Everyone seems to be busy," she said.

"There's a lot to do. Personally, I would rather march out and fight in the open. I don't like being hemmed in. But I guess we don't have that choice now."

Shells from the enemy cannon were thudding against the walls. Some fell into the courtyard. Susannah held her baby tighter as she listened to the noise of the guns.

"War is very loud, isn't it, Davy?"

"Yes, I guess it is. Do you and your baby need anything?"

"No, thank you. Almeron has given us what we need for now. We are as comfortable as can be expected under the circumstances."

# David Crockett

Davy put on his cap and turned to walk away. "Well, if you need something, please let me know."

The sun was setting as Davy walked past Travis's office. Travis called out to him to come in.

"How is Bowie doing?" Travis asked.

"When I left him, he was not feeling very well. I think he is very sick."

Travis shook his head. "That is too bad. I do have respect for him as a fighter. We have some differences, but I would want to be on his side in a fight."

Juan Seguin walked into the room. "You wanted to see me, Colonel?"

"Yes, Juan. I need for you to take a message to Sam Houston for me."

"Colonel Travis, I cannot leave my men. They followed me here. As long as they are staying, I must stay also."

"Juan, I appreciate how you feel. But you can be of great service to those men by going to General Houston and bringing back reinforcements. You know this country better than anyone else here. You have the best chance of getting through to General Houston."

Davy nodded his head. "He is right, Juan. You have seen the number of enemy troops today. We need a lot of men to come here if we are going to stop Santa Anna."

Juan thought for a moment. "My horse is lame. I will need to borrow one."

Travis sat down in his chair. "Jim Bowie has a good horse. He won't be using it for a while. I bet he would let you use his horse."

"All right. I will ask Jim."

"Come back in an hour. It will be dark by then, and I will have the message ready."

Davy watched Juan walk out the door. "He is a brave man, Colonel."

"Yes. I hate to lose him here, but we must get reinforcements, and he has the best chance of bringing them back. Well, I must finish this message. I will talk to you later."

The weather was getting colder as they walked back to their post. The men were roasting some meat over a fire. The meat smelled good, and the warmth of the fire helped take the chill out of the air. One of the men who had come in with Davy called to him as he walked up.

"Hey, Davy. Tell these fellows about the time you grinned that raccoon down from a tree."

Davy sat down by the fire. "Well, it wasn't quite that way. You see, I was out hunting one day and I saw a raccoon up in a tree. Well, I raised old Betsy and pointed it at him. Well sir, that raccoon threw up his hands and said, don't shoot, Davy. I will come down. That raccoon ran down the tree and jumped right in my bag. That beat all I ever saw."

The men laughed as Davy finished his story. Soon Juan came up, leading a horse. Travis was walking beside him.

"Here is the message, Juan. I will have Davy and his men fire at the enemy. That should give you a chance to get away."

Juan mounted his horse. "There is an old trail just north of here. I will head for it, and when I am far enough away, I will swing back to head for General Houston."

Travis shook his hand. "Good luck, Juan. This cold weather should help you. The enemy will be trying to keep warm and not be watching for riders."

Davy and several of his men slipped out of the gate. They began firing at the enemy camp. The enemy fired back, and soon the night was filled with the sound of gunshots. The gate opened once again. Juan rode out and headed toward the road. The children could hear the sound of his horse's hoofbeats. The firing stopped and Davy and his men slipped back into the fort. The sound of the hoofbeats grew fainter and soon they could no longer be heard. The children stared in the direction that Juan had taken. The night was quiet, and dark, and getting very cold.

# Chapter
# Twenty-two

THE COLD NORTH WIND BLEW ACROSS THE TREELESS PRAIRIES, chilling the Alamo defenders as they huddled behind the walls for protection. The children shivered as they held their hands out toward the fire.

"There are more troops marching into town," Davy said as he looked over the wooden fence. "That makes about two or three thousand." He looked around the Alamo. "Sure is a lot more than we have."

None of the men sitting by the fire said anything. They all hoped that Juan Seguin and the other messengers would hurry back with reinforcements. They knew that the small number of men inside the fort could not hold back the large numbers of enemy soldiers marching into San Antonio. A cannon fired, and the men in the Alamo ducked as the shell exploded in the center of the courtyard. Travis walked up as the men were getting off the ground.

"Good morning. How is everyone this morning?"

Davy turned toward Travis. "Not bad. None of my men have been hit by the enemy cannon fire yet."

Travis smiled. "We are very lucky. No one has been hit so far." He walked over and looked across the top of the fence. "I see they have set up a cannon in front of you."

"Yes. They put it in sometime during the night. It must have been after Juan left. I don't think they want any more messengers leaving the Alamo."

Travis pulled out a spyglass and looked at the enemy position. "I hope the messengers we have already sent out will bring us all the reinforcements we need. But I can send some more if we need to."

The enemy band started playing, and enemy soldiers cheered as a man in a bright uniform rode a white horse around the plaza. Davy turned to Travis.

"That must be Santa Anna. I think I will break up his party."

Davy got Betsy and checked to make sure his

powder was dry. He pulled the hammer back and raised the gun to his shoulder. He aimed the gun toward the man riding the white horse.

One of Davy's friends was watching him. "That's a real long shot, Davy."

"I know. I am allowing for the distance and the wind."

A group of men had come over to watch. They made bets on whether or not Davy could shoot Santa Anna at that distance.

"I tell you, if anybody can, it's Davy," one of the men said.

"Even Davy Crockett can't hit a target from this distance," another replied.

Another man spoke up. "You men be quiet. Davy needs to concentrate."

Davy acted like he did not hear the men talking. He gazed down the barrel of the gun and slowly pulled the trigger. The sound of the gunshot made the children jump. Smoke came out of the barrel as the men watched Santa Anna. A few seconds after the shot, the plume on Santa Anna's hat disappeared. The General kicked his horse and rode away as fast as he could. Other enemy soldiers looked around to see who was shooting at them. The men in the Alamo laughed and cheered as they watch Santa Anna gallop away.

"Good shot, Davy," one of the men called.

Davy shook his head. "No. I missed. A gust of wind blew up just as I fired. It blew the bullet off course by that much."

"Well, you sure scared old Santa Anna. I bet he is at home hiding under his bed."

The spirits of the men had been lifted by Davy's shot. They told other men who had not seen it how Davy had shot the plume off Santa Anna's hat and how the general had ridden away. Everyone laughed when they heard the story. Travis put up his spyglass.

"Well, Davy. I think Santa Anna won't be leading any more parades."

Davy shook his head. "I hope I didn't just make him mad."

Travis walked toward his room. Davy turned back to watching the enemy troops.

"That was quite a shot," Dylan said.

Braden nodded his head. "Yes. Santa Anna sure left in a hurry. That was one of the funniest things I have ever seen."

Addie rubbed her hands as she held them toward the fire. "I sure wish the wind would stop blowing. The cold weather is bad enough, but this wind makes it a lot worse. Maybe if it gets cold enough, the enemy army will go home."

"Do you think Davy made Santa Anna mad?" Dylan asked.

Just then a man standing on the wall called down to Travis. "Colonel, the enemy is attacking."

The children watched as the men ran to their places on the wall. Soon they were firing at the attacking enemy.

Addie turned to Dylan. "I guess he made him really mad."

# Chapter
# Twenty-three

ADDIE, DYLAN, AND BRADEN HURRIED AFTER DAVY as he raced to the wall where the men were firing at the advancing enemy army. Davy sprinted up the ladder and stood next to a cannon. The children stood next to him and watched the fighting. Smoke from the rifles and cannon burned their eyes. The smell of the powder filled their nostrils. Men were yelling as they fired. The cannon roared so loudly that the children put their hands over their ears. As the enemy got closer, they could hear them yelling. The bullets from their guns zipped overhead, sounding like angry bees.

Davy moved from man to man. He slapped them on the back and cheered as they fired. The enemy began to slow down. Some of them tried to find a place to hide. Others threw down their muskets and ran to the rear. Finally a bugle sounded and the enemy began to retreat back to their positions. The men in the Alamo cheered as the enemy retreated.

Travis waved his hat in the air. "You have made them run, boys. Hurrah," he cheered. He walked over to Davy. "It was a small attack, but the men did well. I think Santa Anna wanted to get an idea how strong our defenses were. I don't think he will try and attack us like that again."

Davy wiped his face with his sleeve. "I think he will try to soften us up. Look, he is already moving up more cannon. He is going to try to knock some holes in our walls."

Travis watched the enemy begin to dig some new trenches. "I think he will just keep moving closer. When he thinks he has enough men he will attack again. I don't think his whole army is here yet. I hope we get some reinforcements before the rest of his army gets here."

Davy looked beyond the enemy lines. "Do you really think that more men will come?"

Travis shrugged his shoulders. "I hope so."

# David Crockett

The children followed Davy and Travis as they walked around the walls. The men were in good spirits. They thought that the walls were too strong and that the enemy could not get into the Alamo. The cold wind forced most men to duck down behind the walls. They talked quietly about the battle. They nodded and waved as Davy and Travis walked by.

Soon they were standing in front of the wooden fence. Davy's men watched for some sign of an enemy attack. Travis and Davy looked out over the fence.

"Those buildings in front of us are a problem," Travis said. "The enemy can get into them and shoot at us under cover. He can also build up his forces and we can't see them."

Davy stared at the wooden buildings. "You are right. I think the thing to do is to burn them down."

"I agree," Travis said. "After dark, take some men and go burn the buildings down."

"All right. I will pick out a few men, and we will burn down the buildings."

Travis looked at the buildings again.

"Be careful. We can't afford to lose any men."

"I will. If we do it right, we can be down there, set the buildings on fire and get back in here before they know we are doing anything."

Travis looked back at the men cooking in the

courtyard. "I will have the men fire at the enemy from the north wall. That should keep his attention away from you."

"That will be fine, Colonel. Just be sure that they don't shoot us."

"Yell when you start back to the fort. The guards will be watching for you. We will have the gate open."

Travis walked away. Davy walked over to Jim Bowie's room. He knocked on the door. The lady watching Bowie opened the door and peeked out.

"How is he doing, Juana?" Davy asked.

"He was sleeping, but the firing woke him up."

Bowie called out. "Who is it?"

Davy stepped into the room. "It is me, Jim. I came to check on you."

Bowie coughed. "Davy. Good to see you. What is going on?"

"Santa Anna paid us a little visit. We drove him away. The men did well."

"That is what I thought. He will be more careful next time."

"Travis and I decided to burn down those wooden houses outside the walls. They make good cover for the enemy."

"How are you going to do it?" Bowie asked.

"After dark, I am taking some men and we are

going to set them on fire."

Bowie tried to sit up, but he began to cough and he fell back onto his pillow. "Be careful. There will be enemy in those houses."

"How do you know that?" Davy asked.

"Because that is where I would be." Bowie coughed. Juana brought him some water. He drank it and lay back on his cot. "Sorry I can't go with you."

"That's fine, Jim. When you get better and this war is over, we will go hunting together."

Bowie smiled. "I look forward to it."

Davy put his hand on Bowie's shoulder. "I have to go, Jim. I have some houses I need to burn down."

# Chapter
# Twenty-four

IT WAS A DARK NIGHT. Clouds covered the moon. The cold wind still blew, forcing people to take shelter. Davy thought that would be in their favor as he and ten other men prepared to slip out and burn down the houses that provided cover for the enemy. The men waited for the firing on the north wall to begin. Before long the men on the north wall began firing. The enemy returned the fire. Davy and his men lit their torches and ran out of the gate toward the houses.

Addie, Dylan, and Braden followed the men as they ran across the open ground to the first house. Davy motioned for the men to spread out. The men split up and ran to different houses. One of the men threw his torch inside one of the houses. Flames lit up the house as it began to burn. Other houses were set on fire, and soon the flames were making the night bright. Suddenly enemy troops ran out of some of the houses. Davy remembered that Jim Bowie had said they would be there. The enemy started firing at the Texans.

"Get down," Davy shouted. "Return their fire."

The Texans took cover and shot back at the enemy. Bullets were whistling through the air. The children huddled down in a hole and listened to the battle. They could hear the yells of the enemy soldiers as they fired at the Texans. Bullets hit the ground, throwing sprays of dirt on them. They could hear Davy yelling at his men to keep shooting. The burning houses provided enough light that the children could see the enemy as they fired at them.

Addie looked behind her. There was open ground between the Texans and the Alamo. If they tried to run across the open area, the enemy could plainly see them and they would make easy targets. More enemy soldiers were joining the fight. A Texan came running around a building with several enemy chasing him. It looked like the enemy would catch him when the Texans fired at them. The enemy soldiers ran for cover as the Texan joined his friends.

All of the houses were burning. When the enemy tried to put out the fires, the Texans would shoot at them and force them to find a place to hide. Davy looked at his men. They were fighting hard, but they were beginning to run out of ammunition. Davy called to one of his men.

"Antonio."

The man crawled over to Davy.

"We will cover you. Get back to the fort and tell Travis to be ready to cover us when we start back. When he is ready, tell him to fire a cannon at the last house. We will start back then."

Antonio nodded and waited for Davy to give him the signal to start back. Davy told the others to fire as fast as they could. He nodded at Antonio. He ran toward the Alamo as the others fired. The children watched Antonio run across the open ground. Bullets hit all around him. He fell and the children thought he had been shot, but he bounced to his feet and began to run again. Soon he was at the wooden fence. He leaped to the top and other Texans pulled him into the fort.

"He made it, Davy," one of the men yelled.

Davy nodded. "Keep firing. They're still out there."

The Texans kept firing. The noise was so loud, the children could no longer hear the enemy shout. Braden lifted his head.

"The enemy is getting ready to attack. I can see them through the flames."

"You better get down," Dylan yelled. "Those bullets are getting thicker."

One of the men called out, "I am out of bullets, Davy."

"Me too," another said.

Another man pointed to the burning houses. "Davy, the enemy is getting ready to charge."

Davy looked where the man was pointing. He could see the enemy soldiers standing up. Their officers were pointing their swords toward the Texans. Just as the enemy started to move forward, a cannon from the Alamo fired. The cannonball screamed over the heads of the Texans and landed among the enemy soldiers. They dove for cover as Davy called for his men to run toward the Alamo. The men stood up and raced toward the open gate. Enemy bullets hit next to them, making the men run faster. The children ran after the men. Addie was breathing hard as she followed Davy toward the Alamo. It seemed like it was taking forever to cross the open space. Finally they raced through the gate and fell on the ground, gasping for air.

Travis walked over to the group as they started to get up from the ground.

"Good job, men. It will help a lot to have those

houses out of the way."

Davy wiped his face with the sleeve of his shirt. "That was pretty scary out there. Bowie was right. There were enemy soldiers in those houses. I think they were going to attack us in the morning. They would have had good cover if those houses were still there."

He looked back at the burning houses. "Did anybody get hurt?"

Travis smiled. "Not one. I can't believe our good luck. We haven't lost a man yet. I must go write another message. Once again, you did a good job."

Davy walked over and sat next to the wall. The children sat next to him. "That was some fight," Dylan said.

Davy closed his eyes. "Yes it was. The men fought well. I think the enemy knows they have a hard fight in front of them. I just hope the reinforcements get here soon."

Davy stood up and watched the houses burn. "We better get some sleep. There is a lot to do tomorrow."

# Chapter
# Twenty-five

THE DEFENDERS OF THE ALAMO DODGED CANNON SHELLS as they worked to repair the damage to the walls. The enemy cannons fired night and day. It was hard to sleep at night because of the constant shelling. The women and children rarely left their rooms. They huddled indoors, praying for the cannons to stop.

Davy and the children walked across the courtyard. They saw a man coming toward them carrying a keg of gunpowder.

"Morning, Gregorio," Davy called. "Nice day for a stroll."

Gregorio Esparza set the keg of powder down and wiped his forehead.

"Sure is. If you don't mind some falling cannon-balls."

"How is your family doing, Gregorio?" Davy asked.

"They are doing pretty well. They are safe as long as they stay inside. So far they have plenty to eat. My son wants to fight, but he is too young."

"He will probably get his chance someday. Most of us do."

Gregorio nodded. "Yes, it seems there is always someone who wants to rule over everyone else. Santa Anna is a bad man. I do not want my family living in a place where he is the ruler. That is why Antonio and me and the others joined Captain Seguin's company. That is why we came into the Alamo. To make a better place for our families to live."

Some bugles sounded. Davy looked toward the enemy lines. "They keep getting more men all the time. I have lost count of how many they have."

"Yes. They have many men. One of them is my brother. I hope that I do not have to fight him." Gregorio picked up the keg of gunpowder and started to walk away. "I must get this powder to Captain Dickinson. Good-bye, Davy."

# David Crockett

"Good-bye, Gregorio." Davy watched him walk away. "I feel sorry for him. It must be hard to fight against your brother. It just shows how much he wants his family to live in a free land."

The rest of the day was spent strengthening the walls of the Alamo. As the sun set, the men gathered around the fires and cooked their meal. There was little conversation. Most of the men were thinking about their homes and their families.

"The men seem sad tonight, Davy," Addie said.

Just then the enemy band began to play a song. The men in the Alamo could hear it plainly as they sat by their fires.

"What is the name of that song?" Davy asked.

"It is called the Dequello," someone said. "It means that the enemy will give us no mercy."

Davy thought for a minute. He walked over and picked up his fiddle. The children followed him as he walked to another fire.

"Where is John McGregor?" he asked.

A man stood up. "Here I am, Davy. What do you want?"

Davy walked over to McGregor. "Do you hear that music?"

McGregor nodded.

"Well, I think it is bad. It hurts my ears. I hear that

you play the bagpipes."

"That is right," McGregor said.

"I play the fiddle. Maybe not real well, but I can play loud. I think you should get your bagpipes and I will get my fiddle and we will have a contest to see who can play the loudest. What do you boys think?"

The men sitting around the fire laughed and clapped. McGregor smiled.

"I think that is a fine idea. I will be right back."

McGregor walked into a building and soon came out with his bagpipes. He blew into them to warm up then nodded to Davy and began to play. Davy picked up his fiddle, and soon they were making an awful racket. Travis came rushing out of his office and asked, "What is happening?"

"Davy and John are serenading the enemy," someone told him.

Travis smiled and leaned against a wall to listen. Juana came running from the room where she was watching Jim Bowie. She asked someone about the noise, then smiled and walked back inside to tell Bowie what was happening.

Davy and McGregor got louder and louder. The men were laughing and yelling. Some of them got up and began to dance around the fire. Soon the music stopped.

"Don't stop now," the men called.

Davy and McGregor nodded to each other and began playing again. More men began to dance, and soon men were coming from all over the Alamo to listen to the music. Some of the women and children stuck their heads outside to see what was going on. A few women came out and danced with the men. Everyone was having fun. They were no longer thinking about home. The children laughed and clapped as they watched Davy and McGregor. Dylan and Braden tried to dance like the Texans. Everyone seemed to forget that there was an enemy army just outside their walls.

Finally Davy and McGregor stopped playing. Some of the dancers fell to the ground. Others clapped and cheered. The men shouted for more. Davy raised his hand.

"John and I appreciate your knowledge of fine music. But we need some time to catch our breath. I don't know that we can pick a winner of the contest, so we will have to do it another time. Do you agree, John?"

McGregor was breathing heavily. "Yes, Davy. I think we will have to try again."

"Listen," someone said. The men stood quietly in the dark. Finally one of them spoke.

"I don't hear anything."

"That is right. The band stopped. The cannons stopped. They must have been listening to the contest too."

All the men laughed again. Davy raised his hand. "Well, I guess they can't be too bad if they appreciate such good music. I think we all need to get back to our posts now."

The children walked with Davy as he crossed the courtyard. They could feel the happy spirits of the men.

"Davy, you sure made the men feel better," Addie said.

Davy put his hand on her shoulder as they walked. "It made me feel better too. My ears hurt. That bagpipe sounded like a bag full of fighting cats."

Outside the Alamo, a cannon fired and the band began to play again.

# Chapter
# Twenty-six

THE WIND HAD STOPPED BLOWING, but the air was still cold. The men in the Alamo watched the enemy moving their cannon closer. The defenders also scanned the horizon for any sign that help was coming. Davy did all he could to keep the men's spirits high, but it became harder with each passing day. The children followed Davy as he made his rounds each day. He could still get a laugh with his stories. Travis had sent out more messengers, but so far no aid had come.

Addie and the others sat around the fire as the sun set. When it got dark, the band would play and the cannons would fire faster. The men were talking quietly when suddenly a sentry called out.

"Who is there?"

There was no answer, and the sentry called again.

"I said, who is there? Next time I am going to shoot."

Everyone listened. They could hear horses outside the walls. The sentry fired into the darkness. From outside came a shout.

"Hold your fire. We are Texans."

The men rushed to the gate and cheered as some men came riding in. The riders stopped in the middle of the courtyard and got off their horses. One of the men had been shot in the foot by the sentry. Colonel Travis ran from his office, buttoning his jacket as he ran. When he saw the new men, he stopped and quickly counted them. Thirty men. He tried not to look disappointed as he walked to the leader.

"Glad to have you men here. Are others coming?"

The leader shook Travis's hand. "I don't know. We are from Gonzales. We thought others would join us, but we didn't see anyone else."

Travis forced a smile. "Well, if you are here, I am sure others are on the way. Did you have any trouble getting through the enemy lines?"

"No. There is a gap not far from the Gonzales road. We rode right through it."

Travis motioned for the men to follow him. "Come with me. I will show you where the corral is. Then I will take you to your position on the walls."

Davy stood in the circle of defenders, watching the new men. One of them looked familiar. He walked over to the new arrival. "Why, Isaac Millsaps. What are you doing here? Jim Bowie told me he sent you home to take care of your family."

"Yes, he did, Davy. I was with my family when the messenger came saying that the enemy was in San Antonio and Travis needed more men. The men of Gonzales decided to come here, and I joined up with them."

"What about your wife and family?"

"I talked to my wife. She agrees that Texas is the place we want to raise our family. We don't think we will have much of a life if Santa Anna is the ruler. I couldn't let other men go and fight while I stayed home. If Texas is good enough to be my home, it is good enough to fight for. I moved my wife and family into town." Some of the other wives are going to watch after them. I feel better knowing she is not by herself."

Davy slapped Isaac on the back. "We are glad to have you and your friends, Isaac."

Isaac nodded. "I better go put up my horse. I will talk to you later."

Davy watched the Gonzales men lead their horses to the corral. He was talking to some of the defenders when Travis walked up to him.

"I need to talk to you, Davy."

Davy and Travis walked away from the group. "Davy, I must tell you I expected more men to come."

"Well, Colonel, we have thirty more men than we did a little while ago. I think that if these men could make it through the enemy lines, then others can too. Why, pretty soon there will be so many men here that we will have to take turns standing on the wall."

Travis laughed. "I sure hope so. Maybe this is just the first wave of reinforcements. I am sure Colonel Fannin will come. He has several hundred men. He is probably on his way here right now."

"I bet he is. And I bet Sam Houston is coming with more men. I think we should count our blessings that we have not lost any men yet, and that others are coming to join us."

Travis slapped Davy on the back. "You are right. I better make sure the new men are taken care of."

Travis walked away. Dylan looked up at Davy.

"It should make you feel better that these men have come."

Braden nodded. "I think so too. They left their homes and families to be here."

"Yes they did," Davy said. "I think we need to make them feel welcome." He walked toward a group of men standing by a fire. "John McGregor," he called, "where are you? Get your bagpipes. We have some new men to judge our contest."

# Chapter Twenty-seven

SEVERAL DAYS PASSED AND NO OTHER TROOPS CAME. Travis hoped that every day would bring more men. One day as he was walking through the fort, Davy heard a sentry call, "Here comes a rider."

Davy ran to the wall and stood next to Travis. They could see a rider coming fast. He was being chased by enemy cavalry. The rider had a white handkerchief tied around his hat.

"That is James Bonham," Travis called. "I told him to tie a handkerchief around his hat so we would know it was him. Get ready to fire at the enemy."

# David Crockett

The men loaded the cannon and raised their rifles. The enemy was gaining on Bonham when the defenders opened fire on them. The fire from the Alamo caused the enemy to stop chasing Bonham and ride back to their own lines. The Alamo gate opened, and Bonham raced into the courtyard.

Travis and Davy climbed down from the wall and walked with Bonham to Travis's office. The children stood to one side, listening as Bonham made his report.

"Bad news, Colonel. Fannin is not coming. He started, but his wagons broke down and his oxen wandered away, and then he changed his mind about coming. He went back to Goliad."

"Is anybody else coming?" Travis asked.

Bonham shook his head. "Not that I know of."

"Thank you, Jim," Travis said. "Go get some food and some rest."

Travis and Davy watched him leave the office. Travis sat down in his chair. He looked very tired.

"Well, Davy. I guess it is just going to be us. I really believed that people would come to help us."

"So did I," Davy agreed.

The enemy cannon were getting louder. Travis looked at Davy.

"I need to tell the men. They should know that no one is coming."

Davy nodded. "Yes. They should know."

In a short period of time, the men were lined up in the courtyard. The children stood to one side and watched. Susannah Dickinson and the other women watched from the chapel door. Travis left his office and stood in front of the men.

"James Bonham brought bad news today," Travis said. "There are no more reinforcements coming." A low murmur rose from the men. Travis continued. "I have deceived you by telling you that help would come. I did not mean to. I was also deceived by others, who told me that they would come to our aid when the time came. I am here today to give you a choice, to stay or try to escape.

"My own choice is to stay and fight as long as I can. The longer we hold Santa Anna here, the more time it gives General Houston to raise an army to fight him later. But if you choose to leave, you go with my blessings and my thanks. You have done all that was asked of you. All that can be expected of you. Texas should be proud to have men such as you to fight for her."

The men watched as Travis pulled his sword from his scabbard and drew a line in the dirt. When he had drawn the line, he returned to the center of the men.

"All those who are willing to stay and fight with

me for Texas, let them now cross the line."

There was silence as the men considered Travis's words. The children looked at Davy. Slowly a smile crossed his face. He walked across the line and stood next to Travis. A young man named Tapley Holland was the next to cross. Others followed. Slowly at first, then in a rush men crossed Travis's line. Daniel William Cloud, Gregorio Esparza, Isaac Millsaps, Antonio Fuentes, and all the others crossed. Jim Bowie had been brought out on his cot. He raised his head and called to those on the other side of the line.

"Boys, I can't get up. I would appreciate it if you would give me a hand in getting across that line."

Four men ran to the cot and lifted it up. The men cheered as Bowie was carried across the line. The children looked and saw one man still on the other side of the line. His name was Moses Rose. Bowie called out to him.

"Are you not willing to stay with us, Rose?"

Rose shook his head. "No. I am not."

"You might as well stay," Davy said. "You cannot get away."

Rose looked at the brave men standing next to Travis. He turned and looked at the wall.

"I have done worse than to climb that wall," he said.

He walked over and picked up his things. He climbed to the top of the wall and looked back at the men who were watching him. He waved to them, and then jumped down from the wall.

Travis took a few steps out in front of the men.

"Thank you. Now everyone should get back to their posts. We don't know when the enemy will attack."

Travis walked back into his office as the men walked quietly to their places. The children walked quietly next to Davy. They reached the wooden fence and sat down. Addie turned to Davy.

"Why did you stay, Davy? You could have made it through the enemy lines."

Davy smiled. "I must admit I considered it. There is a possibility that I would have escaped. But you know, I have always said, 'be sure you are right', It would not have been right for me to do that. Texas needs me here. I must be willing to do what I can for Texas independence, or I am not worthy to live here. All those other brave men stayed. My place is here with them. Remember, when you are back in school, some things are worth fighting for. Freedom is one of those things."

Davy sat quietly, leaning against the fence. The children were quiet too. They had learned a lesson that could not be taught in school.

# Chapter
# Twenty-eight

"THAT WAS QUITE A SPEECH." Davy looked across the table at Travis.

"I am glad the men decided to stay. I don't know what I would have done if they had all left."

The children sat watching Travis and Crockett talk. The men were at their posts. Most of them were sleeping. The enemy cannon had stopped firing, and the band was not playing.

"Why do you think they stopped firing at us?" Travis asked.

Davy rubbed his eyes. "I think they want us to go

to sleep so when they attack we will not be alert."

"Do you think they will attack soon?"

"I don't know. It seems like they have been out there a long time. I don't even know what day this is."

Travis looked at a little book that was sitting on his desk. "March 6, 1836. It will be the thirteenth day of the siege."

Davy stood up. "I think I will get some sleep. Who knows how long this quiet will las?"

Davy and the children walked outside. Travis lay down on a cot and pulled a blanket around his shoulders. Soon he was asleep.

Outside the Alamo, two thousand enemy soldiers lay on the cold ground. They were waiting for the signal to attack the fort. The soldiers had moved quietly into position several hours before. Now they shivered in the darkness and wished the signal would come. The hours passed, and the soldiers could wait no longer.

One of the soldiers shouted, "Viva, Santa Anna!" The cry was repeated throughout the army. Santa Anna turned to his bugler and ordered him to blow the charge on his trumpet. The bugle notes carried through the darkness. The army rose to its feet and ran toward the Alamo, cheering and yelling.

A sentry on the walls heard the shouts and the pounding of thousands of feet. He turned and yelled,

# David Crockett

"The enemy is attacking!"

In his room, Travis heard the shout and grabbed his shotgun. He rushed outside and raced toward the weak north wall.

"Never surrender, boys!" he yelled as he reached the top of the wall.

Davy jumped to his feet. He looked over the top of the wooden fence. He could see the shapes of the enemy soldiers as they ran toward the Alamo. He raised Betsy to his shoulders and fired. He cheered as he reloaded. The children huddled against the wall. All around them men were firing and yelling. The ground shook when the cannons were fired. The flashes from the cannons and the rifles lit up the Alamo.

The enemy was firing now. The bullets flew over the children's heads. Addie covered her ears. She had never heard such a sound. The boys lay on the ground.

"They are pulling back," someone yelled.

Davy lowered Betsy and wiped the powder from his face. He watched the enemy soldiers pull back out of range of the Texans' rifles. The men were cheering.

"It is not over. They will be back," Davy warned.

Just then the bugle sounded and the enemy rushed toward the Alamo once again. The firing was just as loud as it was the first time. Screams and cheers blended with the sound of guns as the defenders fought to keep the enemy out of the Alamo. The children watched Davy. He yelled at the enemy as he reloaded. He had a fierce look in his eye. He dared the enemy to charge his fence.

Once more the enemy pulled back. Once more the Alamo defenders cheered. One of the men turned to Davy. "If we can keep them out a little longer maybe they will quit," he said.

Davy nodded, but did not say anything. The bugle sounded once again.

"Here they come!" a man yelled.

Once more the enemy raced toward the Alamo. Davy and his men fired as fast as they could. Some of the enemy moved toward other parts of the walls. Soon there was a great mob of enemy soldiers at the foot of the north wall. Travis shot down into the mass of soldiers. The enemy at the foot of the wall fired back. Addie looked across the courtyard toward the north wall. She saw Travis fall from the wall and lay still on the ground.

"They are climbing over the wall," Dylan said.

Some enemy soldiers had climbed the wall and were now racing across the courtyard. The men on the walls turned to fire at them. This allowed other soldiers to climb up the walls, and soon the enemy was inside the fort. The enemy soldiers opened the gates, and more men rushed inside the Alamo.

Braden watched as a group of soldiers entered the room where Jim Bowie was lying on his bed. He heard two pistol shots and the sound of a struggle. Soon the enemy soldiers came walking out of the room. One of them carried Bowie's knife.

"We have to pull back to the chapel," Davy called to his men.

The children stayed close to Davy as he and his men fought their way through the enemy toward the Alamo chapel. There was not time to reload now so Davy swung Betsy like a club. The enemy soldiers tried to stay out of Davy's way as he moved across the courtyard. Davy looked down and saw the children.

"You must go now," he said.

"How?" Addie asked.

"Back through the tunnel of light," Davy answered.

The children turned and saw a tunnel of light in the middle of the courtyard.

"Run for the tunnel," Davy said as he swung Betsy at the charging enemy.

Addie looked at Davy. "Good-bye, Davy." She turned and ran after Dylan and Braden, who were entering the tunnel. She could see enemy soldiers running all around the courtyard. She looked behind her. A soldier was running after her, his arm reaching for her. Just before she reached the tunnel she felt a hand grab her shoulder and pull her back. She saw the tunnel closing as she fought the hand on her shoulder.

# Chapter
# Twenty-nine

"ADDIE. WAKE UP."

Addie felt the hand on her shoulder, shaking her. She looked up expecting to see the face of an enemy soldier. Instead she saw her mother looking at her. She looked at the other people standing in the room. There were two people in uniform who must be security. Another lady looked over her mother's shoulder. Dylan and Braden stood next to the lady.

"Are you all right?" her mother asked.

Addie nodded her head. She looked around the room. It was the storeroom she and the boys had entered. The one where they had met Davy.

"I am fine," she said. "What happened?"

Her mother helped her stand up. "You and the boys must have fallen asleep. I guess you came in here and the door locked when it shut. You should not have gone into strange buildings."

The lady who was watching Addie said, "This is an old storeroom. Nobody comes in here. You are lucky that we found you. It is nearly time to close the Alamo. You could have been here all night."

Addie looked at Dylan and Braden. They were smiling at her. "Mother, we met Davy Crockett. He was right here in this room. He took us through a tunnel of light and we saw his whole life. We were here in the Alamo when the enemy attacked. I was running to get back to the light tunnel when a soldier grabbed my shoulder. I thought that was him shaking me. I am so glad it was you."

Addie's mother stroked her hair. "You just had a dream. We found all of you sleeping here. I was so worried when I came to pick you up and you were not here. This nice lady and these guards helped me look for you. We were about to give up when we found this building."

Addie looked around. "You mean there was no tunnel of light and no Davy? But I saw him. Dylan,

Braden, didn't you see him?"

The boys nodded.

The grownups laughed. Addie's mother took her hand. "You were here to find information on Davy Crockett for a school paper. You all just dreamed about what you were trying to find."

"But it was so real," Addie said as she walked out of the building with her mother.

"We will go home and have a nice dinner. Then tomorrow you and the boys can work on your paper."

Addie walked away with her mother and the others. She stopped and looked back at the small building. The door was cracked open. She saw a shadowy figure smiling at her from behind the door. The figure took off his coonskin cap and waved to her. Addie turned to tell the others, but they had walked around a corner. She turned back to the building, but the door was shut and the building was dark and quiet.

Check out these other fine titles by
Durban House at your local book store.

Exceptional Books
by
Exceptional Writers

# FICTION

## NONFICTION

## DURBAN HOUSE FICTION

A DREAM ACROSS TIME                                    Annie Rogers
    Jamie Elliott arrives from New York onto the Itish Caribbean island
of St. Lucia, and finds herself caught tip in Island forces, powerful across the
centuries, which Find deep echoes in her recurring dreams.

AFTER LIFE LIFE                                          Doti Goldman
    A hilarious murder mystery taking place in the afterlife. Andrew
Law, Chief Justice of the Texas Supreme Court, is the picture of robust
health when he suddenly dies. Upon arriving in the afterlife, Andy discovers
he was murdered, and his untimely has death has soule some unexpected
and far-reaching consequences—a worldwide depression, among others.
Many diabolical plots are woven in this funny, fast-paced whodunit, with a
surprising double-cross ending.

an-eye-for-an-eye.com                                   Dennis Powell
    Jed Warren, Vietnam Peacenik, and Jeff Porter, ex-Airborne, were
close friends and executives at Megafirst Bank. So when CFO McAlister
crashes the company, creams off millions in bonuses, and wipes out Jed and
Jeff, things began to happen.
    If you wonder about corporate greed recorded in today's newspapers,
read what one man did about it in this intricate, devious, and surprise-
ending thriller

BASHA John Hamilton Lewis
    LA reviewer, Jeff Krieder's pick as "Easily my best read of the year."
Set in the world of elite professional tennis, and rooted in ancient Middle
East hatreds of identity and blood loyalties, Basha is charged with the fiercely
competitive nature of professional sports, and the dangers of terrorism.
An already simmering Middle East begins to boil, and CIA Station Chief
Grant Corbet must track down the highly successful terrorist, Basha. In a
deadly race against time Grant hunts the elusive killer only to see his worst
nightmare realized.

THE BEIRUT CONSPIRACY                                  John R. Childress
    At some point every person is faced with a moral dilemma: the right
choice or the easy choice. The Beirut Conspiracy is a fast-paced thriller torn
from today's headlines. For newly elected US President Roswell Pierce, world

peace or uncontrollable global terrorism wait his decision. For drunken and disbarred physician Matthew Richards, his time as a student in Beirut is about to catch up with him, forcing him into an equally difficult choice.

THE CORMORANT DOCUMENTS                    Robert Middlemiss
        Who is Cormorant, and why is his coded letter on Hitler's stationary found on a WWI Nazi bomber preserved in the Arctic? And why is the plane loadedwith Goering's plundered art treasures? Mallory must find out or die. On the run front the British Secret Service and CIA, he finds himself caught in a secret that dates back to 1945.

CRISIS PENDING                                  Stephen Cornell
        When U.S. oil refineries blow up, the White House and the Feds move fast, but not fast enough. Sherman Nassar Ramsey, terrorist for hire, a loner, brilliant, multilingual, and skilled with knives, pistols, and bare hands, moves around the country with contempt, case and cunning.
        As America's fuel system starts grinding to a halt, rioting breaks out for gasoline, and food becomes scarce, events draw Lee Hamilton's wife, Mary, into the crisis. And when Ramsey kidnaps her, the battle becomes very personal.

DANGER WITHIN                                   Mark Danielson
        Over 100 feet down in cold ocean waters lies the wreck of pilot Kevin Hamilton's DC- 10. In it are secrets which someone is desperate to keep. When the Navy sends a team of divers from the Explosives Ordinance Division, a mysterious explosion from the wreck almost destroys the salvage ship. The FBI steps in with Special Agent Mike Pentaglia. Track the life and death of Global Express Flight 3217 inside the gritty world of aviation, and discover the shocking cargo that was hidden on its last flight.

DEADLY ILLUMINATION                             Serena Stier
        It's summer 1890 in New York City. A ebullient young woman, Florence Tod, must challenge financier, John Pierpont Morgan, to solve a possible murder. J.P's librarian has ingested poison embedded in an illumination of a unique Hildegard von Bingen manuscript. Florence and her cousin, Isabella Stewart Gardner, discover the corpse. When Isabella secretly removes a gold tablet from the scene of the crime, she sets off a chain of events that will involve Florence and her in a dangerous conspiracy.

DESIGNED TO KILL                                          Chester D. Campbell
        Award winning author Chester Campbell brings back Greg McKenzie
and his wife, Jill, to the glistening white beaches at Perdido Key, Florida.
Tim Gannon, son of the McKenzies's closest friends, has been found dead
of a gunshot wound. 'Self-inflicted,' says the deputy who investigated, a
clear case of remorse over the design flaw in a highrise beachfront condo
that caused a balcony to collapse, killing two people. But, after two thugs
work Greg over, he realizes Jill is in danger too, and if this is a murder case,
he had better solve it fast.

HANDS OF VENGEANCE                                           Richard Sand
        Private detective Lucas Rook returns still haunted by the murder
of his twin brother. What seems like an easy case involving workplace
violations, the former homicide detective finds himself locked in a life and
death struggle with the deadly domestic terrorist group, The Brothers of the
Half Moon. A must-read for lovers of dark mysteries.

HORIZON'S END                                               Andrew Lazarus
        This wide-ranging international novel presents on man's long haunted
pursuit of abandoned values on three continents—North America, Europe,
and Asia. Through it all, the wartime sounds of Morse Code signals remind
him of his journalist's mission to keep the faith and reveal the truth. Jack
Lerner often finds himself in the arms of women who are brilliant, sultry,
and enigmatic. He fights his fight facing tough decisions in honest news
reporting and contending with a family's survival in a world that refuses to
live up to his own personal moral standards.

HOUR OF THE WOLVES                                    Stephatic Daimlen-Völs
        After more than three centuries, the Poisons Affair remains one
of history's great, unsolved mysteries. The worst impulses of human
nature—sordid sexual perversion, murderous intrigues, witchcraft, Satanic
cults—thrive within the shadows of the Sun King's absolutism and will
culminate in the darkest secret of his reign; the infamous Poisons Affair, a
remarkably complex web of horror, masked by Baroque splendor, luxury
and refinement.

A HOUSTON WEEKEND                                           Orville Palmer
        Professor Edward Randall, not-yet-forty, divorced and separated
from his daughters, is leading a solitary, cheerless existence in a university

town. At a conference in Houston, he runs into his childhood sweetheart. Then she was poverty-stricken, American Indian. Now she's elegantly attired, driving an expensive Italian car and lives in a millionaires' enclave. Will their fortuitous encounter grow into anything meaningful?

THE INNOCENT NEVER KNEW                           Mark W. Danielson
When Senator Sam Tinsdale's plane crashes short of the runway during a snowstorm and city-wide power failure, NTSB investigator is sent to Albuquerque to investigate. But when he arrives, he finds the crash site tampered with, evidence removed, and is threatened by men in snowsuits who refuse to provide I.D. When his boss, Ralph Dietz, issues a statement that the Cockpit Voice Recorder and Flight Data Recorder had failed, Stambler smells a cover-up.

JOHNNIE RAY AND MISS KILGALLEN                   Bonnie Hearn Hill
                                                      and Larry Hill
Based on the real-life love affair between 1950's singer Johnnie Ray and columnist Dorothy Kilgallen. They had everything—wealth, fame, celebrity. The last thing they needed was love. Johnnie Ray and Miss Kilgallen is a love story that travels at a dangerous, roaring speed. Driven close to death from their excesses, both try to regain their lives and careers in a novel that goes beyond the bounds of mere biography.

THE LAST COWBOYS                              Robert E. Hollmann
What do you do when you have outlived your time?
Clint and Bubba, two aging cowboys, bodies worn out from rodeos and ranching, whose best days are behind them, try and survive in a citified world. Follow The Last Cowboys as they fight modern society in an attempt to hold on to the way of life they know and love.

THE LATERAL LINE                              Robert Middlemiss
Kelly Travert was ready. She had the Israeli assassination pistol, she had coated the bullets with garlic, and tonight she would kill the woman agent who tortured and killed her father. When a negotiator for the CIA warns her, suddenly her father's death is not so simple anymore.

LETHAL CURE                                        Kurt Popke
Dr. Jake Prescott is a resident on duty in the emergency room when medics rush in with a double trauma involving patients sustaining injuries

during a home invasion. Jake learns that one patient is the intruder, the other, his wife, Sara. He also learns that his four-year-old daughter, Kelly, is missing, and his patient may hold the key to her recovery.

A MEETING OF MINDS                           Elizabeth Turner Calloway
Treachery…passion…conflict…denial…betrayal   swirl   through
A Meeting of Minds like a Texas tornado. Against the backdrop of the glamour world of meetings and conventions, a young Dallas mother strives to save herself and the family business from the clutches of a charming but scheming man.

THE MEDUSA STRAIN                                    Chris Holmes
Finalist for Fore Word Magazine's 'Book of the Year'. A gripping tale of bio-terrorism that stunningly portrays the dangers of chemical warfare. Mohammed Ali Ossman, a bitter Iraqi scientist who hates America, breeds a deadly form of anthrax, and develops a diabolical means to initiate an epidemic. It is a story of personal courage in the face of terror, and of lost love found.

MR. IRRELEVANT                                        Jerry Marshall
Booklist Star Review. Chesty Hake, the last man chosen in the NFL draft, has been dubbed Mr. Irrelevant. By every yardstick, he should not be playing pro football, but because of his heart and high threshold for pain, he endures. Then during his eighth and final season, he slides into paranoia, and football will never be the same.

NO ORDINARY TERROR                                J. Brooks Van Dyke
In this elegant and meticulously researched Edwardian detective story, J. Brooks Van Dyke brings to life the stylized fashions and customs of the time, and weaves across them a story of treason, medicine, and murder. Follow Richard and Emma Watson, nephew and niece to the Watson of Sherlock Holmes fame, as they explore dangerous leads into aristocratic mansions and London's filthiest slums.

OPAL EYE DEVIL                                   John Hamilton Lewis
"Best historical thriller in decades." Good Books. In the age of the Robber Baron, Opal Eye Devil weaves an extraordinary tale about the brave men and women who risk everything as the discovery of oil rocks the world. The richness and pageantry of two great cultures, Great Britain

and China, are brought together in a thrilling tale of adventure and human relationships.

PRIVATE JUSTICE                                              Richard Sand
    Ben Franklin Award 'Best Mystery of the Year'. After taking brutal revenge for the murder of his twin brother, Lucas Rooks leaves the NYPD to become a private eye. A father turns to Rook to investigate the murder of his daughter. Rook's dark journey finds him racing to find the killer, who kills again and again as Private Justice careens toward a startling end.

ROADHOUSE BLUES                                          Baron R. Birtcher
    From the sun-drenched sands of Santa Catalina Island to the smoky night clubs and back alleys of West Hollywood, Roadhouse Blues is a taut noir thriller. Newly retired Homicide detective Mike Travis is torn from the comfort of his chartered yacht business into the dark, bizarre underbelly of Los Angeles's music scene by a grisly string of murders.

RUBY TUESDAY                                             Baron R. Birtcher
    When Mike Travis sails into the tropical harbor of Kona, Hawaii, he expects to put LA Homicide behind him. Instead, he finds the sometimes seamy back streets and dark underbelly of a tropical paradise and the world of music and high finance, where wealth and greed are steeped in sex, vengeance, and murder.

SAMSARA                                              John Hamilton Lewis
    A thrilling tale of love and violence set in post-World War Hong Kong. Nick Ridley, a captain in the RAF, is captured and sent to the infamous Japanese prisoner-of-war camp, Changi, in Singapore. He survives brutal treatment at the hands of the camp commandant, Colonel Tetsuro Matashima. Nick moves to Hong Kong, where he reunites with the love of his life, Courtney, and builds a world-class airline. On the eve of having his company recognized at the Crown Colony's official carrier, Courtney is kidnapped, and people begin to die. Nick is pulled into the quagmire, and must once again face the demon of Changi.

SECRET OF THE SCROLL                               Chester D. Campbell
    Finalist 'Deadly Dagger' award, and ForeWord Magazine's 'Book of the Year' award. Deadly groups of Palestinians and Israelis struggle to gain possession of an ancient parchment that was unknowingly smuggled from

Israel to the U.S. by a retired Air Force investigator. Col. Greg McKenzie finds himself mired in the duplicitous world of Middle East politics when his wife is taken hostage in an effort to force the return of the first century Hebrew scroll.

SECRETS ARE ANONYMOUS                                    Frederick L. Cullen
A comic mystery with a cast of characters who weave multiple plots, puzzles, twists, and turns. A remarkable series of events unfold in the lives of a dozen residents of Bexley, Ohio. The journalism career of the principle character is derailed when her father shows up for her college graduation with his boyfriend on his way to a new life in California.

THE SEESAW SYNDROME                                      Michael Madden
A terrifying medical thriller that slices with a scalpel, exposing the greed and corruption that can happen when drug executives and medical researchers position thernselves for huge profits. Biosense Pharmaceuticals has produced a drug named Floragen, and now they need to test it on patients to gain FDA approval. But there's a problem with the new drug. One of the side effects included death.

THE SERIAL KILLER'S DIET BOOK                            Kevin Postupack
Finalist ForeWord Magazine's 'Book of the Year' award. Fred Orbis is fat, but he dreams of being Frederico Orbisini, internationally known novelist, existential philosopher, raconteur, and lover of women. Both a satire and a reflection on morals, God and the Devil, beauty, literature, and the best-seller list, The Serial Killer's Diet Book is a delightful look at the universal human longing to become someone else.

THE STREET OF FOUR WINDS                                 Andrew Lazarus
Paris, just after World War II. A time for love, but also a time of political ferment. In the Left Bank section of the city, Tom Cortell, a tough, intellectual journalist, finally learns the meaning of love. Along with him is a gallery of fascinating characters who lead a merry and sometimes desperate chase between Paris, Switzerland, and Spain in search of themselves.

TAINTED ANGELS                                           Greg Crane
"One of the best mafia thrillers in years."
Tainted Angels tells the story of a Chicago crime family that defeats the Israeli underground's incursion into the New York drug market. After

succeeding in New York, Mario Paterlini, with the help of his three sons, expand their narcotics empire in California, where he must deal with the CIA, Mexican drug lords, an Italian narcotics broker, and Los Angeles gangs.

TERMINAL CARE                                    Arvin Chawla
Billionaire Thomas Poole, Sr., does not believe his son died from an overdose. As he watches the life support being pulled from Michael's body, he wants vengeance, and not on any street-level punks. A fast, scary thriller that will make you think twice about that next hospital stay.

TUNNEL RUNNER                                    Richard Sand
A fast, deadly espionage thriller peopled with quirky and sometimes vicious characters, Tunnel Runner tells of a dark world where murder is committed and no one is brought to account, where loyalties exist side by side with lies and extreme violence.

WHAT GOES AROUND                                 Don Goldman
Finalist ForeWord Magazine's 'Book of the Year' award. Ray Banno, a medical researcher, was wrongfully incarcerated for bank fraud. What Goes Around is a dazzling tale of deception, treachery, revenge, and nonstop action that resolves around money, sex, and power. The book's sharp insight and hard-hitting style builds a high level of suspense as Banno strives for redemption.

## DURBAN HOUSE NONFICTION

BEHIND THE MOUNTAIN:                          Nick Williams
A CORPORATE SURVIVAL BOOK
A harrowing true story of courage and survival. Nick Williams is alone, and cut off in a blizzard bchind the mountain. In order to survive, Nick called upon his training and experience that made him a highly successful business executive. In Behind the Mountain: A Corporate Survival Book, you will find the finest practical advice on how to handle yourself in tough spots, be they life threatening to you, or threatening to your job performance or the company itself. Read and learn.

FISH HEADS, RICE, RICE WINE & WAR       LTC. Thomas G. Smith
                                                          (Ret.)
A human, yet humorous, look at the strangest and most misunderstood war ever, in which American soldiers were committed. Readers are offered an insiders view of American life in the midst of highly deplorable conditions, which often lead to laughter.

JIMMY CARTER AND THE RISE                   Philip Pilevsky
OF MILITANT ISLAM
One of America's foremost authorities oil the Middle East, Philip Pilevsky argues that President Jimmy Carter's fallure to support the Shah of Iran led to the 1979 revolution. That revolution legitimized and provided a base of operations for militant Islamists across the Middle East. A most thought provoking book.

MIDDLE ESSENCE...                               Landy Reed
WOMEN OF WONDER YEARS
A wonderful book by renowned speaker Landy Reed that shows how real women in real circumstances have confronted and conquered the obstacles of midlife. This is a must have guide and companion to what can be the most significant and richest years of a woman's life.

PROTOCOL                                   Mary Jane McCaffree,
(25th Anniversary Edition)                    Pauline Innis, and
                                                Richard Sand
Protocol is a comprehensive guide to proper diplomatic, official and social usage. The Bible for foreign governments, embassies, corporations,

public relations firms, and individuals wishing to do business with the Federal Government. "A wealth of detail on every conceivable question, from titles and forms of address to ceremonies and flag etiquette." Department of State Newsletter.

SPORES, PLAGUES, HISTORY:                          Chris Holmes
THE STORY OF ANTHRAX
"Much more than the story of a microbe. It is the tale of history and prophecy woven into a fabric of what was, what might have been and what might yet be. What you are about to read is real—you are not in the Twilight Zone—adjusting your TV set will not change the picture. However, it is not hopeless, and we are not helpless. The same technology used to create biological weapons can protect us with better vaccines and treatments." CDR. Ted J. Robinson, U.S. Navy Epidemiologist.

WHAT MAKES A MARRIAGE WORK?                          Malcolm D. Mahr
You hear the phrase "marry and settle down," which implies life becomes more serene and peaceful after marriage. This simply isn't so. Living together is one long series of experiments in accommodation. What Makes a Marriage Work? is a collection of fifty insights reflecting one couple's searching, experimenting, screaming, pouting, nagging, whining, moping, blaming, and other dysfunctional behaviors that helped them successfully navigate the turbulent sea of matrimony for over fifty years. (Featuring 34 New Yorker cartoons of wit and wisdom.)

WHITE WITCH DOCTOR                          John A. Hunt
A true story of life and death, hope and despair in apartheid-ruled South Africa. White Witch Doctor details white surgeon John Hunt's fight to save his beloved country in a time of social unrest and political upheaval, drawing readers into the world of South African culture, mores and folkways, superstitions, and race relations.